Campaigning

Campaigning
U.S. Marines Corps

FMFM 1-1

GOVERNMENT REPRINTS PRESS
Washington, D.C.

© Ross & Perry, Inc. 2001 All rights reserved.

No claim to U.S. government work contained throughout this book.

Protected under the Berne Convention. Published 2001

Printed in The United States of America
Ross & Perry, Inc. Publishers
717 Second St., N.E., Suite 200
Washington, D.C. 20002
Telephone (202) 675-8300
Facsimile (202) 675-8400
info@RossPerry.com

SAN 253-8555

Government Reprints Press Edition 2001

Government Reprints Press is an Imprint of Ross & Perry, Inc.

Library of Congress Control Number: 2001092428

http://www.GPOreprints.com

ISBN 1-931641-15-3

♾ The paper used in this publication meets the requirements for permanence established by the American National Standard for Information Sciences "Permanence of Paper for Printed Library Materials" (ANSI Z39.48-1984).

All rights reserved. No copyrighted part of this publication may be reproduced, stored in a retrieval system, or transmitted, in any form or by any means, electronic, photocopying, recording, or otherwise, without the prior written permission of the publisher.

DEPARTMENT OF THE NAVY
Headquarters United States Marine Corps
Washington, D.C. 20380-0001

25 January 1990

FOREWORD

Tactical success in combat is not enough, because tactical success of itself does not guarantee victory in war. History has proved this. What matters ultimately in war is success at the level of strategy, the level directly concerned with attaining the aims of policy. That these two levels of war are connected and that there is an art to the way tactical results are used to advance the strategic purpose are beyond doubt. With this thought as its point of departure, *this book discusses this intermediate operational level which links strategy and tactics, describing the military campaign as the primary tool of operational warfare.*

This book, *Campaigning*, thus establishes the authoritative doctrinal basis for military campaigning in the Marine Corps, particularly as it pertains to a Marine Air-Ground Task Force (MAGTF) conducting a campaign or contributing to a campaign by a higher authority. *Campaigning* is designed to be in consonance with FMFM 1, *Warfighting*, and presumes understanding of the philosophy described therein. In fact, *Campaigning* applies this warfighting philosophy specifically to the operational level of war. Like FMFM 1, this book is descriptive rather than prescriptive in nature; it requires judgment in application.

Chapter 1 provides a conceptual discussion of the campaign and the operational level of war, their relationship to strategy and tactics, and their relevance to the Marine Corps. In many situations, the MAGTF clearly has operational—vice merely tactical—capabilities; therefore it is essential that Marine leaders learn to think operationally. Chapter 2 describes the considerations and the mental process for developing a campaign. *This mental process, and the strategic vision it derives from, are essential to success at the operational level.* Chapter 3 discusses the operational considerations vital to conducting a campaign, examining in detail the differences between tactical and operational activities.

Central to this book is the idea that military action, at any level, must ultimately serve the demands of policy. Marine leaders at all levels must understand this point and must realize that tactical success does not exist for its own sake. The importance of this understanding is particularly evident in conflicts at the low end of the intensity spectrum—the revolutionary warfare environment—where military force is not the dominant characteristic of the struggle but is only one of several components of national power, all of which must be fully coordinated with one another. *In a campaign Marine leaders must therefore be able to integrate military operations with the other elements of national power in all types of conflict.*

This book makes frequent use of familiar historical examples to put its concepts into concrete terms. *But do not be deceived into thinking this is a history book with little relevance to the challenges facing today's Marine Corps.* These are classical examples intended to illustrate principles with enduring and universal application. Many future crises will be "short-fuzed" and of limited duration and scale. *But make no mistake; no matter what the size and nature of the next mission—whether it be general war, crisis response, peacekeeping, nation building, counterinsurgency, counterterrorism, or counternarcotics operations—the concepts and the thought process described in this book will apply.*

This manual is designed primarily for MAGTF commanders and their staffs and for officers serving on joint and combined staffs. However, the method described here for devising and executing a progressive series of actions in pursuit of a distant objective in the face of hostile resistance and the broad vision that this demands apply equally to commanders at all levels. *Therefore, as with FMFM 1, I expect all officers to read and reread this book, understand its message, and apply it. Duty demands nothing less.*

A. M. GRAY
General, U.S. Marine Corps
Commandant of the Marine Corps

DISTRIBUTION: 139 000060 00

FMFM 1-1

Campaigning

Chapter 1. The Campaign
Strategy – Tactics – Operations – Strategic-Operational Connection – Tactical-Operational Connection – Interaction of the Levels – Campaigns – Battles and Engagements – Strategic Actions – The Marine Corps and Campaigning

Chapter 2. Designing the Campaign
Strategic Aim, End State, and Operational Objectives – Identifying Critical Enemy Factors – The Concept – Conceptual, Functional, and Detailed Design – Sequencing – Direction – Campaign Plan

Chapter 3. Conducting the Campaign
Strategic Orientation – Use of Combat – Perspective – Maneuver – Mobility – Tempo – Intelligence – Surprise – Logistics – Leadership

Conclusion

Notes

As used in this book, the terms **operations** and **operational** refer specifically to the operational level of war and not to military actions in the general sense.

Chapter 1

The Campaign

"Battles have been stated by some writers to be the chief and deciding features of war. This assertion is not strictly true, as armies have been destroyed by strategic operations without the occurrence of pitched battles, by a succession of inconsiderable affairs."[1]

—Baron Henri Jomini

"For even if a decisive battle be the goal, the aim of strategy must be to bring about this battle under the most advantageous circumstances. And the more advantageous the circumstances, the less, proportionately, will be the fighting. The perfection of strategy would be, therefore, to produce a decision without any serious fighting."[2]

—B.H. Liddell Hart

"It is essential to relate what is strategically desirable to what is tactically possible with the forces at your disposal. To this end it is necessary to decide the development of operations before the initial blow is delivered."[3]

—Field-Marshal Bernard Montgomery

FMFM 1-1 —————————————— The Campaign

This book is about military campaigning. A campaign is a series of related military actions undertaken over a period of time to achieve a specific objective within a given region. Campaigning reflects the operational level of war, at which the results of individual tactical actions are combined to fulfill the needs of strategy.

In this chapter we will describe how events at different levels of war interact, focusing on the operational level as the link between strategy and tactics. We will examine the campaign as the basic tool of commanders at the operational level, and we will discuss its relevance to the Marine Corps.

STRATEGY

Civil policy creates and directs war. Thus, Liddell Hart wrote, "any study of the problem ought to begin and end with the question of policy."[4] The activity that strives directly to attain the objectives of policy, in peace as in war, is strategy. At the highest level, the realm of grand strategy,[5] this involves applying and coordinating all the elements of national power—economic, diplomatic, psychological, technological, military. Military strategy is the applied or threatened use of military force to impose policy.[6] Military strategy must be subordinate to grand strategy and should be coordinated with the use of the other elements of national power, although historically neither has always been so. U.S. military strategy is applied regionally by the unified commanders in chief of the various theaters of war. Military strategy will likely be combined strategy, the product of a coalition with allies.

In war, military strategy involves the establishment of military strategic objectives, the allocation of resources, the imposition of conditions on the use of force, and the development of war plans. We can describe military strategy as the discipline of winning wars. The means of military strategy are the components of military power. Its ways are the strategic concepts[7] devised for the accomplishment of its end, the policy objective.

Military strategy is the province of national policymakers, their military advisors, and the nation's senior military leadership — seemingly far beyond the professional concern of most Marines.

Tactics

Marines are generally most familiar and comfortable with the tactical realm of war, which is concerned with defeating an enemy force at a specific time and place.[8] The tactical level of war is the world of combat. The means of tactics are the various components of combat power at our disposal. Its ways are the concepts by which we apply that combat power against our adversary. These are sometimes themselves called tactics—in our case, tactics founded on maneuver. Its end is victory: defeating the enemy force opposing us. In this respect, we can view tactics as the discipline of winning battles and engagements.

The tactical level of war includes the maneuver of forces in contact with the enemy to gain a fighting advantage, the application and coordination of fires, the sustainment of forces throughout combat, the immediate exploitation of success to seal the victory, the combination of different arms and weapons, the gathering and dissemination of pertinent combat information, and the technical application of combat power within a tactical action—all to cause the enemy's defeat. Although the events of combat form a continuous fabric of activity, each tactical action, large or small, can generally be seen as a distinct episode contested over a limited field of battle and span of time.

Tactical success of itself does not guarantee victory in war. In modern times, the result of a single battle is seldom sufficient to achieve strategic victory, as it often was in Napoleon's time. In fact, a single battle alone can rarely resolve the outcome of a campaign, much less an entire war. One example in which a single tactical victory did end a campaign ironically demonstrates that tactical victory does not necessarily even result in strategic advantage. Robert E. Lee's costly tactical victory at Antietam in 1862 was an operational defeat in that it compelled him to abort his offensive campaign into the North. Even a succession of tactical victories, taken together, often does not ensure strategic victory, the obvious example being the American experience in the war in Vietnam. Thus, we must recognize that *to defeat the enemy in combat cannot be an end in itself, but rather must be viewed as a means to a larger end.*

OPERATIONS

It follows that there exists a discipline of the military art above and distinct from the realm of tactics but subordinate to the lofty domain of strategy. This discipline is called operations (or the operational level of war), and it is the link between strategy and tactics.[9] The aim at this level is to give meaning to tactical actions in the context of some larger design, which itself ultimately is framed by strategy. Put another way, the aim is to get strategically meaningful results through tactics.

The operational level of war thus consists of the discipline of conceiving, focusing, and exploiting a variety of tactical actions to realize a strategic aim. In its essence, the operational level involves deciding when, where, for what purpose, and under what conditions to give battle—and to refuse battle as well—with reference to the strategic design. It governs the deployment of forces, their commitment to or withdrawal from combat, and the sequencing of successive tactical actions to achieve strategic objectives.[10]

The nature of these tasks implies that the commander has a certain amount of latitude in the conception and execution of plans. "The basic concept of a campaign plan should be born in the mind of the man who has to direct that campaign."[11] If execution is prescribed by higher authority, he is merely the tactical executant, as in the case of Air Force and Navy forces conducting the 1986 air strike against Libya.

The basic tool by which the operational commander translates tactical actions into strategic results is the campaign. Thus as strategy is the discipline of making war, and tactics is the discipline of fighting and winning in combat, we can describe the operational level of war as the discipline of campaigning. Its means are tactical results—be they victories, losses, or draws. Its end is the accomplishment of the established strategic aim. Its ways are the schemes by which we combine and sequence the tactical means to reach the strategic end.

STRATEGIC-OPERATIONAL CONNECTION

Strategy must be clearly understood to determine the conduct of all military actions. But we must understand as well that the strategy-operations connection is a two-way interface. Just as strategy shapes the design of the campaign, so must strategy adapt to operational circumstances. Failure to adapt results in a strategy that is ignorant of operational reality, such as Napoleon's ill-fated war of 1812 against Russia, in which "the problems of space, time and distance proved too great for even one of the greatest military minds that has ever existed."[12]

Strategy guides operations in three basic ways: it establishes aims, allocates resources, and imposes conditions on military action.[13] Together with the enemy and the geography of the theater or area, strategic guidance defines the parameters of operations.[14]

First, strategy translates policy objectives into military terms by establishing military strategic aims. It is important to keep in mind that these aims will likely be but one component of a broader grand strategy. The overriding criterion for the conduct of a campaign is the reference, direct or derivative, to the strategic aim. The operational commander's principal task is to determine and pursue the sequence of actions that will most directly serve that aim.[15]

Strategists must be prepared to modify aims as they reevaluate costs, capabilities, and expectations. When strategic aims are unreasonable, the operational commander must so state. When they are unclear, he must seek clarification. While required to pursue the established aim, he is obliged to communicate the associated risks.[16]

Second, strategy provides resources, both tangible resources such as material and personnel and intangible resources such as political and public support for military operations.[17] When resources are insufficient, the operational commander must seek additional resources or request modification of the aims.[18]

Third, strategy, because it is influenced by political and social concerns, places conditions on the conduct of military operations. These conditions take the form of restraints and constraints. Restraints prohibit or restrict certain military actions, such as the prohibition imposed on MacArthur in Korea against bombing targets north of the Yalu River in 1950 or Hitler's order (arguably in the hope of gaining a favorable negotiated peace with Great Britain) putting a temporary halt on the overrunning of France in 1940. Restraints may be constant, as the laws of warfare, or situational, as rules of engagement. Constraints, on the other hand, obligate the commander to certain military courses of action—such as Hitler's insistence that Stalingrad be held, which resulted in the loss of the Sixth German Army in 1943, or the political demand for a symbol of American resolve which necessitated the defense of Khe Sanh by the 26th Marines in 1968, although the position was of questionable military significance. Similarly, strategy may constrain the commander to operations which gain rapid victory, such as Germany's need to defeat Poland quickly in 1939 so to be able to turn to face the western Allies or Abraham Lincoln's perceived need to end the American Civil War quickly lest Northern popular resolve falter.

When limitations imposed by strategy are so severe as to prevent the attainment of the established aim, the commander must request relaxation of either the aims or the limitations. But we should not be automatically critical of conditions imposed on operations by higher authority, since "policy is the guiding intelligence"[19] for the use of military force. However, no senior commander can use the conditions imposed by higher authority as an excuse for military failure.[20]

TACTICAL-OPERATIONAL CONNECTION

Stemming from strategic guidance, operations assist tactics by establishing focus and goals. In that manner, operations provide the context for tactical decision making. Without this operational coherence, warfare at this level is reduced to a series of disconnected and unfocused tactical actions with relative attrition the only measure of success or failure.[21]

Just as operations must serve strategy by combining tactical actions in such a way as to most effectively and economically achieve the aim, they must also serve tactics by creating the most advantageous conditions for our tactical actions. In other words, we try to shape the situation so that the outcome is merely a matter of course. "Therefore," Sun Tzu said, "a skilled commander seeks victory from the situation and does not demand it of his subordinates."[22] And just as we must continually interface with strategy to gain our direction, we must also maintain the flexibility to adapt to tactical circumstances as they develop, for tactical results will impact on the conduct of the campaign. As the campaign forms the framework for combat, so do tactical results shape the conduct of the campaign. In this regard, the task is to exploit tactical victories to strategic advantage and to minimize, nullify, or even reverse the strategic effect of tactical losses.

Operations imply broader dimensions of time and space than do tactics, because the strategic orientation at this level forces the commander to broaden his perspective beyond the limits of immediate combat.²³ While the tactician fights the battle, the operational commander must look beyond the battle. In advance he seeks to shape events to create the most favorable conditions possible for those combat actions he chooses to fight. Likewise he seeks to anticipate the results of combat and to be prepared to exploit them to the greatest strategic advantage.

The operational level of war is sometimes described as the command of large military units. Indeed, at its upper limits, it is the province of theater commanders. However, it is erroneous to define the operational level according to echelon of command. Large is a relative term; in general, the larger the scale and complexity of a war, the higher the echelons of command performing at the operational level. For example, in a conventional conflict in central Europe, the corps commander may very well be the lowest-level operational commander. However, in a small war the operational conduct of war will take place at a much lower echelon. "Regardless of size, if military force is being used to achieve a strategic objective, then it is being employed at the operational level."²⁴

INTERACTION OF THE LEVELS

The levels of war form a definite hierarchy. The technical application of combat power is subordinate to the needs of tactical combat, just as tactical actions merely compose the parts of a campaign, which is itself but one phase of a strategic design for gaining the objectives of policy. While there exists a clear hierarchy, there are no sharp boundaries between the levels, which tend rather to merge together. As all the levels share the same purpose of serving the ends set down by policy, the difference is one of scale rather than principle.

Consequently, a particular echelon of command is not necessarily concerned with only one level of war. A theater commander's concerns are clearly both strategic and operational. A MAGTF commander's responsibilities will be operational in some situations and largely tactical in others and may actually span the transition from tactics to operations in still others. A commander's responsibilities within the hierarchy depend on the scale and nature of the war and may shift up and down as the war develops.

Actions at one level can often influence the situation at others. Edward Luttwak calls this the interpenetration[25] of levels, in which results at one level can, in part or whole, dictate results at another. Harmony among the various levels tends to reinforce success, while disharmony tends to negate success. Failure at one level tends naturally to lessen success at the next higher level. This is fairly obvious.

Less obvious is the phenomenon that the manner of success at one level may also negate success at higher levels—as British reprisals in the Carolinas in 1780 fanned the dying embers of revolution into open flame; many of the patriotic troops at the battles of King's Mountain and Cowpens were local militia not imbued with any particular revolutionary fervor but fighting only to protect their homes against the depredations of British forces. Or, imagine a government whose strategy is to quell a growing insurgency by isolating the insurgents from the population but whose military tactics cause extensive collateral death and damage. The government's tactics alienate the population and make the insurgent's cause more appealing, strengthening the insurgent strategically.

Brilliance at one level may to some extent overcome shortcomings at another, but rarely can it overcome incompetence. Operational competence can rarely overcome the tactical inability to perform, just as strategic incompetence can squander what operational success has gained.

The natural flow of influence in the hierarchy is from the top down; that is, it is much easier for strategic incompetence to squander operational and tactical success than it is for tactical and operational brilliance to completely overcome strategic incompetence or disadvantage. The Germans are generally considered to have been tactically and operationally supreme in two world wars, but the obstacle of strategic incompetence proved insurmountable. Conversely, outgunned and overmatched tactically, the Vietnamese Communists nonetheless prevailed strategically.

But the flow can work in reverse as well; brilliance at one level can overcome, at least in part, shortcomings at a higher level. In this way the tactical and operational abilities of the Confederate military leaders held off the overwhelming strategic advantage of the North for a time — until Lincoln found a commander who would press that strategic advantage. Similarly, Erwin Rommel's tactical and operational flair in North Africa in 1941-42 transcended for a time Britain's strategic advantage. Interestingly, this operational flair was coupled with a strategic shortsightedness in another example of interaction among the levels. Rommel's ambitious campaigning in a theater that was clearly of subsidiary importance had the ultimate effect of drawing German attention and resources from more important theaters.[26]

What matters finally is success at the level of strategy, for it is the concerns of policy which are the motives for war in the first place and which determine success or failure. The important lesson is not to be able to discern at what level a certain activity takes place or where the transition occurs between levels, but to ensure that from top to bottom and bottom to top all activities in war are coordinated and focused. Further, we should never view the tactical realm of war in isolation, for the results of combat become relevant only in the larger context of the campaign. The campaign, in turn, only gains meaning in the context of strategy.

A Comparative Case Study: GRANT VERSUS LEE

A comparative examination of the strategic, operational, and tactical methods of Generals Ulysses S. Grant and Robert E. Lee during the American Civil War offers an interesting illustration of the interaction of the levels. Popular history regards Grant as a butcher and Lee a military genius. But a study of their understanding of the needs of policy and the consistency of their strategic, operational, and tactical methods casts the issue in a different light. [27]

POLICY

The North faced a demanding and complex political problem, namely "to reassert its authority over a vast territorial empire, far too extensive to be completely occupied or thoroughly controlled."[28] Furthermore, Abraham Lincoln, recognizing that Northern popular resolve might be limited, established rapid victory as a condition as well. Lincoln's original policy of conciliation having failed — as translated into a military strategy for limited war by General George McClellan — the President opted for the unconditional surrender of the South as the only acceptable aim. His search for a general who would devise a strategy to attain his aim ended with Grant in 1864. By comparison, the South's policy aim, Southern independence having already been declared, was simply to prevent the North from succeeding, to make the endeavor more costly than the North was willing to bear.

MILITARY STRATEGY

Grant's strategy was directly supportive of the established policy objectives. He recognized immediately that his military strategic aim must be the destruction of Lee's army, and he devised a strategy of annihilation focused resolutely on that aim. General George Meade's Army of the Potomac was to lock horns with Lee's Army of Northern Virginia, battling relentlessly—"Lee's army will be your objective point. Wherever he goes, there you will go also."[29] Similarly, he gave his cavalry commander, General Philip Sheridan, "instructions to put himself south of the enemy and follow him to the death. Wherever the enemy goes, let our troops go also."[30] Meanwhile, General William Sherman was to sweep out of the west in a strategic envelopment into Lee's rear. Consistent with the policy objective of ending the war as rapidly as possible, Grant initiated offensive action simultaneously on all fronts to close the ring quickly around his opponent. His order shortly after assuming command terminating the common practice of prisoner exchanges, which was a vital source of manpower for the Confederates, demonstrated a keen appreciation for the larger situation. Satisfied that he had finally found a commander who could translate policy into a successful military strategy, Lincoln wrote Grant in August 1864: "The particulars of your plans I neither know nor seek to know. . . . I wish not to obtrude any restraints or constraints upon you."[31]

The South's policy objectives would seem to indicate a military strategy of attrition based on prolonging the war as a means to breaking Northern resolve—as had been George Washington's strategy in the Revolution. In fact, this was the strategy preferred by Confederate President Jefferson Davis. Such a strategy would involve Lee's dispersal of his army into the greatest possible expanse of territory. Lee, however, chose to concentrate his army in Virginia. This was due in part to a perspective much narrower than Grant's and the fact that he was constrained to defend Richmond. But it was due also to Lee's insistence on offensive strategy—not merely an offensive-defensive as in the early stages of the war, but eventally an ambitious offensive strategy in 1862 and '63 aimed at invading the North as a means to breaking Northern will. Given the South's relative weakness, Lee's strategy was questionable at best[32]—both as a viable means of attaining the South's policy aims and also in regard to operational practicability, particularly the South's logistical ability to sustain offensive campaigns.

OPERATIONS

Consistent with his strategy of grinding Lee down as quickly as possible and recognizing his ability to pay the numerical cost, Grant aggressively sought to force Lee frequently into pitched battle, which he accomplished by moving against Richmond in such a way as to compel Lee to block him.

Even so, it is unfair to discount Grant as nothing more than an unskilled butcher. "He showed himself free from the common fixation of his contemporaries upon the Napoleonic battle as the hinge upon which warfare must turn. Instead, he developed a highly uncommon ability to rise above the fortunes of a single battle and to master the flow of a long series of events, almost to the point of making any outcome of a single battle, victory, draw, or even defeat, serve his eventual purpose equally well."[33]

Lee, on the other hand, had stated that, being the weaker force, his desire was to avoid a general engagement.[34] But in practice, he seemed unable to resist the temptation of a climactic battle of Napoleonic proportions whenever the enemy was within reach. By comparison, General Joseph Johnston in the west seemed to better appreciate the need for a protracted conflict. "He fought a war of defensive maneuver, seeking opportunities to fall upon enemy detachments which might expose themselves and inviting the enemy to provide him with such openings, meanwhile moving from one strong defensive position to another in order to invite the enemy to squander his resources in frontal attacks, but never remaining stationary long enough to risk being outflanked or entrapped."[35] Between Chattanooga and Atlanta, while suffering minimal casualties, Johnston had held Sherman to an average advance of a mile a day. Of Johnston's campaign, Grant himself had written: "For my own part, I think that Johnston's tactics were right. Anything that could have prolonged the war a year beyond the time that it did finally close, would probably have exhausted the North to such an extent that they might have abandoned the contest and agreed to a separation."[36]

TACTICS

Lee's dramatic tactical successes in battles such as Second Manassas, Chancellorsville, and Antietam speak for themselves. But neither Lee nor Grant can be described tactically as particularly innovative. In fact, both were largely ignorant of the technical impact of the rifled bore on the close-order tactics of the day, and both suffered high casualties as a result.[37] However, due to the relative strategic situations, Grant could better absorb the losses that resulted from this tactical ignorance than could Lee, whose army was being bled to death. In this way, Grant's strategic advantage carried down to the tactical level.

While Grant's activities at all levels seem to have been mutually supporting and focused on the objectives of policy, Lee's strategy and operations appear to have been, at least in part, incompatible with each other and with the requirements of policy and the realities of combat. In the final analysis, Lee's tactical flair could not overcome operational and strategic shortcomings. In fact, it proved irrelevant; even tactical victories such as Antietam became operational defeats.

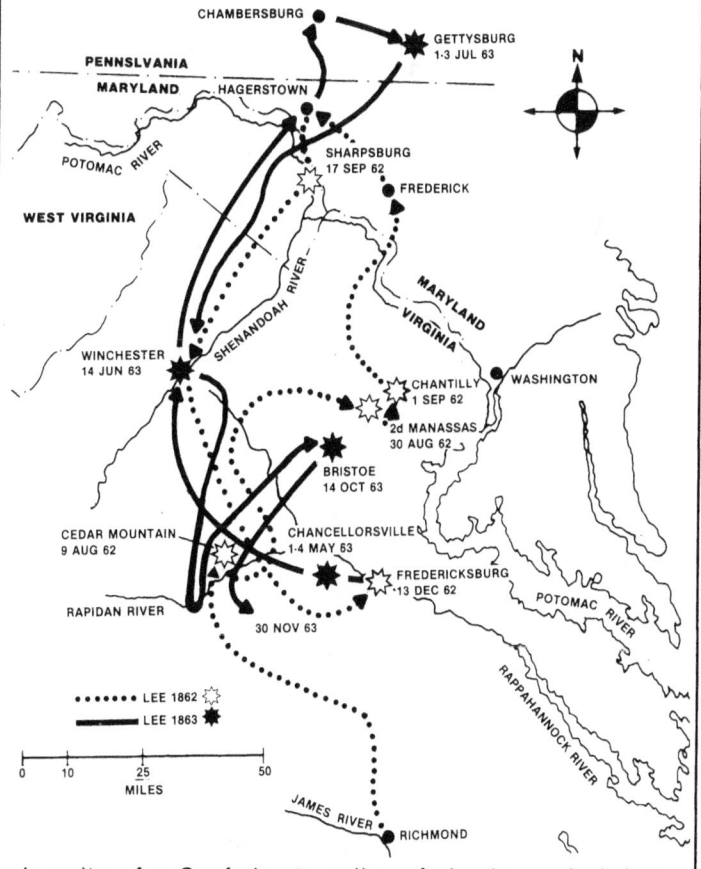

Campaigns at odds with strategy: LEE, 1862-63

In spite of a Confederate policy of simple survival, Lee adopts an ambitious offensive strategy comprising two campaigns of invasion which fail in their strategic purpose.

Campaigns supporting strategy: GRANT, 1864-65

Compatible with the Federal aim of rapid unconditional victory, Grant devises an all-encompassing strategy of annihilation which includes the relentless attack of Lee and the loosing of Sherman into Lee's rear.

The Wilderness to Appomattox: GRANT, 1864-65

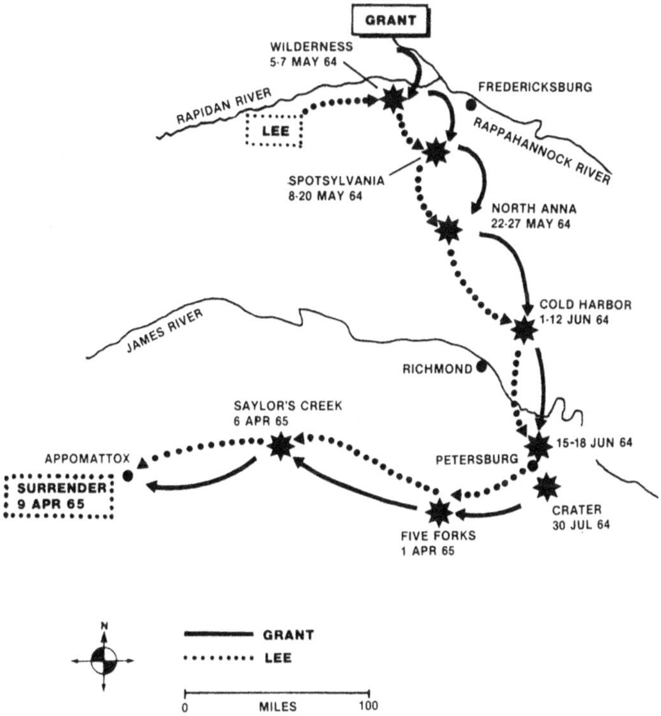

Grant clearly defines his aim: the destruction of Lee's army. He attacks relentlessly, maneuvering against Richmond to compel Lee to fight him. Grant's instructions to Meade: "Lee's army will be your objective point. Wherever he goes, there you will go also."

Campaigns

As we have seen, the principal tool by which the operational commander pursues the military conditions that will achieve the strategic goal is the campaign. Campaigns tend to take place over the course of weeks or months, but they may encompass years. They may vary drastically in scale, from large campaigns conceived and controlled at the theater or even National Command Authority level to smaller campaigns conducted by task forces within a larger command. Generally, each campaign has a single strategic objective. If there is more than one strategic objective in a theater, campaigns are waged sequentially or simultaneously.

In that way, minor campaigns may exist within larger ones. For example, the Allied Pacific campaign during the Second World War comprised subordinate campaigns by General Douglas MacArthur in the southwest Pacific, Admiral William Halsey in the south Pacific, and Admiral Chester Nimitz in the central Pacific. Halsey's campaign in the south Pacific itself included a smaller campaign in the Solomon Islands which lasted five months and comprised operations from Guadalcanal to Bougainville.

Battles and Engagements

A battle is an extensive tactical fight between sizable combat forces. Battles generally last days, sometimes weeks. They occur when adversaries commit to fight to a decision at a particular time and place for a significant objective. Consequently, battles are usually of operational significance, if not necessarily operationally decisive. But this is not always the case; the Battle of the Somme in 1916, which was actually a series of inconclusive battles over the span of four and a half months, had the net effect of moving the front some eight miles while exacting over 600,000 casualties on each side.

An engagement is a combat between opposing forces on a scale of magnitude less than that of a battle. Several engagements may compose a battle. Engagements may or may not be operationally significant, although the object, of course, is to turn the result to operational advantage.

Battles and engagements are the physical clashes that make up the hard points[38] of a campaign. They generally provide the campaign its shape; at the same time the campaign gives them meaning. This is not to say that campaigns are merely a succession of tactical clashes, nor even that these clashes are the chief and deciding features of a campaign. A campaign may be characterized as much by the lack of battle; for example, General Nathanael Greene versus Lord Cornwallis in North Carolina in 1781. For six weeks Greene led the battle-thirsty Cornwallis on a wearying chase through the North Carolina countryside. Only after the British force had been "worn to a frazzle,"[39] did Greene agree to battle. The Revolutionaries were driven from the field, but the British were so exhausted after the chase that in spite of the tactical victory they were forced to withdraw to the coast.

We have mentioned before, but it bears repeating, that to defeat the enemy in battle is not an end in itself, but a means to an end—unless the operational concept is simply to gain the strategic end by attrition, as was the U.S. strategy in Vietnam.[40] The true object is to accomplish the aim of strategy with the minimal amount of necessary combat, reducing "fighting to the slenderest possible proportions."[41]

We do not mean to say that we can, or should, avoid all fighting. How much fighting we do will vary with the strength, skill, and intentions of the opponent as well as our own. War being a violent enterprise, clashes will occur. The ideal is to give battle only where we want and when we must—when we are at an advantage and have something important to gain we cannot gain without fighting. But, understanding that we are opposed by a hostile will with ideas of his own, we recognize that we will not always have this option. Sometimes we must fight at a disadvantage: when faced with an unfavorable meeting engagement, when ambushed, when simply forced to by a skilled enemy, or when strategic obligations constrain us (such as an inability to give ground—NATO's current plan for the forward defense of Germany, for example).

STRATEGIC ACTIONS

As we have seen, tactical actions gain strategic significance only when placed in the construct of a campaign. Strategic actions, on the other hand, by definition bear directly on strategic objectives, although their magnitude and duration are less than those of a campaign. Examples of strategic actions include the 1983 invasion of Grenada to restore order and evacuate U.S. medical students, the truck-bombing of the Marine headquarters by a single Shi'ite at the Beirut airport in the same year, and the 1986 punitive U.S. airstrike against Libya. Actions need not be of large scale to have strategic impact.[42]

Due to their very nature, strategic actions are normally conceived at the national level, at which they may also be planned and directed. However, planning and execution may also be delegated to the theater or even task force level. If such actions are controlled at senior levels, the operational commander tasked with execution will have little latitude in the manner of execution.

Strategic actions sometimes include special operations. As their name implies, special operations may require forces that are specially trained or equipped. But it is important to keep in mind that what makes these actions operations is not elite units or the specialized equipment they use.

Rather, it is the effective employment of forces toward the achievement of specific objectives of strategic significance.

THE MARINE CORPS AND CAMPAIGNING

Having described the interaction of the levels of war and introduced the campaign, we must ask ourselves what its relevance is to the Marine Corps. We can answer this question from several angles. Organizationally, the MAGTF is uniquely equipped to perform a flexible variety of tactical actions, amphibious, air, and land, and to focus those actions into a united scheme. The MAGTF's organic aviation allows the commander to project power well in advance of close combat, to shape events in time and space. The headquarters organization, with separate headquarters for the tactical control of ground and air actions, can free the MAGTF command element to focus on the operational conduct of war.

From a conventional employment angle, a MAGTF may be the first American ground force at the scene of a crisis in an undeveloped theater of operations where no command structure is in place. In that case, the MAGTF commander's responsibilities will rest firmly in the operational realm— regardless of the size of the MAGTF. Even in a developed theater, a MAGTF may be required to conduct a campaign in pursuit of a strategic objective as part of a larger maritime campaign or as part of a larger land campaign by a Joint Task Force (JTF). In some cases, the MAGTF may itself be the JTF headquarters. Perhaps most important, a MAGTF commander must be prepared to articulate the most effective operational employment of his MAGTF in a joint or combined campaign. If he cannot, he will in effect depend on the other services to understand fully the capabilities of the MAGTF and employ it correctly, an assumption which is likely to prove unwarranted.

A less conventional perspective offers further reasons the operational level is important to Marines. The importance of strategic actions has led the Marine Corps to designate some units special operations-capable. As we have determined, to be special operations-capable, a unit must be able to function operationally. While lacking the scope and duration of a campaign, such operations share the campaign's strategic orientation.

Further, the changing nature of war resulting from the emergence of the electronic media offers another reason for understanding the operational level of war. Television by its range and influence on popular opinion can work operationally; that is, it can often elevate even minor tactical acts to higher importance. Consequently, all Marines must understand how tactical action impacts on strategy, which is the essence of war at the operational level.

Finally, regardless of the echelon of command or scale of activity, even if it rests firmly in the tactical realm, the methodology described here—devising and executing a progressive plan in pursuit of a distant goal and deciding when and where it is necessary to fight for that goal—applies.

Chapter 2

Designing the Campaign

"No plan survives contact with the enemy."[1]
— Field Marshal Helmuth von Moltke ("The Elder")

"By looking on each engagement as part of a series, at least insofar as events are predictable, the commander is always on the high road to his goal."[2]
— Carl von Clausewitz

"To be practical, any plan must take account of the enemy's ability to frustrate it; the best chance of overcoming such obstruction is to have a plan that can be easily varied to fit the circumstances met; to keep such adaptability, while still keeping the initiative, the best way is to operate along a line which offers alternative objectives."[3]
— B.H. Liddell Hart

Designing the Campaign

Having defined and described the operational level of war and its principal weapon, the campaign, we will now discuss the mental process and the considerations involved in designing a campaign. In this respect, the commander's key responsibility is to provide focus[4] — by his campaign design to fuse a variety of disparate tactical acts, extended over time and space, into a single, coalescent whole. It is important to note at the outset that due to the inherently uncertain and disordered nature of war, campaign design is of necessity a continuous and fluid process, as Moltke reminds us.

STRATEGIC AIM, END STATE, AND OPERATIONAL OBJECTIVES

The design should focus all the various efforts of the campaign resolutely on the established theater strategic aim. Economy is an essential ingredient in campaign design. Any activity or operation which does not contribute, directly or derivatively, in some necessary way to this aim is unjustifiable. Of course, the aim may shift over time, for a variety of reasons — including the success, failure, or cost of the unfolding campaign itself — and we must continuously adjust our design appropriately. This focus on the military strategic aim is the single overriding element of campaign design.

This notion is reflected in U.S. Grant's strategy for the Civil War as described in his memoirs:

> The armies were now all ready for the accomplishment of a single object. They were acting as a unit so far as such a thing was possible over such a vast field. Lee, with the capital of the Confederacy, was the main end to which all were working. Johnston, with Atlanta, was an important obstacle in the way of accomplishing the result aimed at, and was therefore almost an independent objective. It was of less importance only because the capture of Johnston and his army would not produce so immediate and decisive a result in closing the rebellion as would the possession of Richmond, Lee, and his army. All other troops were employed exclusively in support of these two movements.[5]

Given the strategic aim as our destination, our next step is to determine the desired end state, the military conditions we must realize in order to reach that destination, those necessary conditions which we expect by their existence will provide us our established aim. Grant envisioned these conditions to be the destruction of Lee's army and the capture of Richmond. These conditions will vary with the nature of the conflict and need not always consist of the destruction of the enemy. In fact, the lethality of modern weapons may necessitate the adoption of limited aims, such as protecting a region, denying or capturing enemy war resources, curbing or limiting enemy influence, diverting enemy resources from more important theaters or areas, or deterring enemy aggression.

FMFM 1-1 — Designing the Campaign

In the main, the more general the conflict, the more predominant are the military factors, and the easier it is to translate aims into military terms. The unconditional surrender of the enemy as a policy aim translates easily into the outright defeat of his military forces: "You will enter the continent of Europe and, in conjunction with other Allied Nations, undertake operations aimed at the heart of Germany and the destruction of her Armed Forces."[6] But the more limited the aims of conflict, the less predominantly military is the conduct of the war, and the more difficult it is to translate those aims into military conditions, as illustrated by the questionable military mission of Marine forces in Beruit 1982-84.

From the envisioned end state, we can develop the operational objectives which, taken in combination, will achieve those conditions. In Grant's concept, the defeat of Joseph Johnston and the capture of Atlanta were important operational objectives. It is important to note that as the strategic aim shifts, so must our determination of the conditions of success and operational objectives shift as well.

IDENTIFYING CRITICAL ENEMY FACTORS

We must anticipate that the enemy will do everything within his power to interfere with our attaining our aims. Therefore, we must plan to deal with the enemy in such a way that foils his ability to interfere. Our design must focus on critical enemy factors, and the ability to do this depends on an accurate estimate of the situation.

  Economy demands that we focus our efforts toward some object or factor of decisive importance in order to achieve the greatest effect at the least cost. The most effective way to defeat our enemy is to destroy that which is most critical to his success in the theater. Clearly, we should focus our efforts against an object of strategic importance since this will have the greatest effect. Failing the ability to do that, we focus against objects of operational importance.[7] In other words, we should strike him where and when we can hurt him most, or, as Sun Tzu said, "Seize something he cherishes and he will conform to your desires."[8] Returning to the example of Grant in the Civil War, while his aim was the defeat of Lee, the critical factor on which this hinged was Sherman's campaign into the heart of the South. This is reflected in Grant's instructions to Sherman in April 1864: "You I propose to move against Johnston's army, to break it up and to get into the interior of the enemy's country as far as you can, inflicting all the damage you can against their war resources."[9]

  We obviously stand a better chance of success by acting against enemy vulnerability rather than against strength. In some cases, these vulnerabilities may be of critical importance, such as the maldeployment of forces at the outset of a campaign, insufficient air defenses, or comparatively poor operational mobility. We should search for and exploit such critical vulnerabilities directly. By using multiple simultaneous thrusts or initiatives, we may identify these vulnerabilities more quickly.

Often, a factor is critical to the enemy because it represents a capability he cannot do without. It is a source of strategic or operational strength. Clearly, if we can destroy such a critical capability we can weaken our enemy severely. But we do not want to attack this capability directly, strength versus strength; rather, we prefer to attack it from an aspect of vulnerability or even to preempt it before it becomes a strength (such as to delay by air power the junction of enemy forces in order to defeat a superior foe piecemeal). Critical capabilities may be immediately vulnerable to attack; for example, by means of a choke point at which we can sever the enemy's line of operation. However, the enemy will likely recognize the importance of this capability and will take measures to protect it. Thus, a critical capability may not be directly vulnerable. We may have to create vulnerability: we may have to design a progressive sequence of actions to expose or isolate the critical capability, perhaps focusing on lesser capabilities and vulnerabilities en route, creating by our actions over time the opportunity to strike the decisive blow.

Just as we ruthlessly pursue our enemy's critical factors, we should expect him to attack ours, and we must take steps to protect them over the course of the campaign. This focus on critical factors as they bear at the operational level, from both our and the enemy's points of view, is central to campaign design.

THE CONCEPT

Having established, at least temporarily, the aim and having identified those critical factors which we believe will lead most effectively and economically to the enemy's downfall, we must develop a concept or scheme which focuses on these factors in pursuit of the aim. This is the truly creative aspect of campaign design and of the military art in general: conceiving an original overall scheme for success, attuned to the complex set of particulars which make each situation unique.[10]

The concept captures the essence of the design and provides the foundation from which spring the more mechanical aspects of campaign design. It encompasses our broad vision of what we plan to do and how we plan to do it. Our intent, clearly understood and explicitly stated, therefore must be an integral component of the concept. Our concept should also contain in general terms an idea of when, where, and under what conditions we intend to give and refuse battle.

FMFM 1-1 — Designing the Campaign

The concept should demonstrate a certain boldness, which is in itself "a genuinely creative force."[11] It should demonstrate a ruthless focus on critical enemy factors. It should exhibit creativity and novelty; avoid discernible conventions and patterns; make use of artifice, ambiguity, and deception; and reflect, as Churchill wrote, "an original and sinister touch, which leaves the enemy puzzled as well as beaten."[12] It should create multiple options, so that we can adjust to changing events and so that the enemy cannot discern our true intent. And it should provide for speed in execution, which is a weapon in itself.

History is replete with examples at all levels of a superior idea as the basis for notable success: Hannibal's concept of a thin center and heavy wings, which enabled his rout of Varro at Cannae; Grant's plan for fixing Lee near Richmond and loosing Sherman through the heart of the South; the conceptual marriage of infiltration tactics with mechanization which became the blitzkrieg in 1940; the idea of bypassing Japanese strongholds which became the basis for the island-hopping campaigns in the Second World War in the Pacific; MacArthur's bold concept of a seaborne, operational envelopment to topple the North Korean advance, which became the Inchon landing in 1950; and the idea of eliminating the Viet Cong guerrillas' support base by pacifying the South Vietnamese villages, which was the basis for the generally successful but short-lived Combined Action Program.

Conceptual, Functional, and Detailed Design

We can describe this conceiving of an overall scheme for accomplishing our goal as conceptual design. Conceptual design becomes the foundation for all subsequent design, which we can call functional design and detailed design.[13] These are the more mechanical and routine elements of campaign design which are concerned with translating the concept into a complete and practicable plan. Functional design is, just as the name implies, concerned with designing the functional components necessary to support the concept: the subordinate concepts for logistics, deployment, organization, command, intelligence, fire support, sequencing. Functional design provides for the general characteristics and conditions required by the concept. Detailed design encompasses the specific planning activities necessary to ensure that the plan is coordinated: movements, landing tables, deployment or resupply schedules, communications plans, reconnaissance plans, control measures, specific command relationships. Detailed design should not become so specific, however, that it inhibits flexibility. Mindful of Moltke's dictum, we must recognize that any plan, no matter how detailed, is simply a common basis for change.

It should be clear that no amount of subsequent planning can reduce the requirement for an overall concept. But while we must clearly recognize that conceptual design becomes the foundation for functional and detailed design, we must also recognize that the process works in the other direction as well. Our concept must be receptive to functional realities. Functional design in turn must be sensitive to details of execution. In this way, the realities of deployment schedules (a functional concern) can dictate employment schemes (a conceptual concern). Likewise, logistical requirements shape the concept of operations—logistics becomes the tail that wags the dog. Campaign design thus becomes a continuous, two-way process aimed at harmonizing the various levels of design activity.

Sequencing

Given a strategic aim not attainable by a single tactical action at a single place and time, we design a campaign comprising several related phases sequenced over time to achieve that aim. Phases are a way of organizing the extended and dispersed activities of the campaign into more manageable parts which allow for flexibility in execution. "These phases of a plan do not comprise rigid instructions, they are merely guideposts. . . . Rigidity inevitably defeats itself, and the analysts who point to a changed detail as evidence of a plan's weakness are completely unaware of the characteristics of the battlefield."[14]

An excellent example is General Dwight Eisenhower's broad plan for the recapture of Europe in the Second World War,

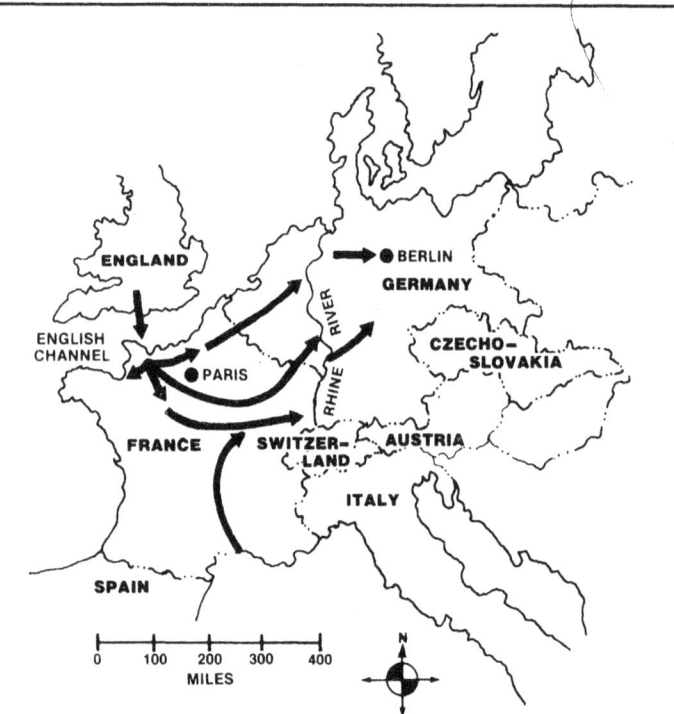

Phases of a Campaign: EISENHOWER, 1944-45

The phases of Eisenhower's broad design for the reconquest of Europe in the Second World War, as originally conceived. His directive from the Combined Chiefs of Staff: "You will enter the continent of Europe and, in conjunction with the other Allied Nations, undertake operations aimed at the 'heart of Germany and the destruction of her Armed Forces."

which described, in his words, "successive moves with possible alternatives":

> Land on the Normandy coast.
>
> Build up resources needed for a decisive battle in the Normandy-Brittany region and break out of the enemy's encircling positions. (Land operations in the first two phases were to be under the tactical direction of Montgomery.)
>
> Pursue on a broad front with two army groups, emphasizing the left to gain necessary ports and reach the boundaries of Germany and threaten the Ruhr. On our right we would link up with the forces that were to invade France from the south.
>
> Build up our new base along the western border of Germany, by securing ports in Belgium and in Brittany as well as in the Mediterranean.
>
> While building up our forces for the final battles, keep up an unrelenting offensive to the extent of our means, both to wear down the enemy and to gain advantages for the final fighting.
>
> Complete the destruction of enemy forces west of the Rhine, in the meantime seeking bridgeheads across the river.
>
> Launch the final attack as a double envelopment of the Ruhr, again emphasizing the left, and follow this up by an immediate thrust through Germany, with the specific direction to be determined at the time.
>
> Clean out the remainder of Germany.[15]

Eisenhower remarked that "this general plan, carefully outlined at staff meetings before D-Day, was never abandoned, even momentarily, throughout the campaign."[16]

Phases may occur simultaneously as well as sequentially. Each phase may be a single operation or, in the case of large campaigns, a minor campaign in itself. The phases of a campaign are the parts which, taken in proper combination, compose the operational whole. Our task is to devise the operational combination of actions which most effectively and quickly achieves the strategic aim. This means far more than simply the accumulation of tactical victories, which we have already concluded is no guarantee of strategic success.

While each phase may be generally distinguishable from the others as a distinct episode, it is necessarily linked to the others and gains significance only in the larger context of the campaign. As demonstrated in the example above, the manner of distinction may be separation in time or space or a difference in aim or forces assigned. We should view each phase as an essential component in a connected string of events, related in cause and effect. Like a chess player, we must learn to think beyond the next move, looking ahead several moves and considering the long-term effects of those moves and how to exploit them. In this way, each phase has an envisioned sequel or potential sequels.[17] "The higher commander must constantly plan, as each operation progresses, so to direct his formations that success finds his troops in proper position and condition to undertake successive steps without pause."[18] And like a chess player, we cannot move without considering the enemy's reactions or anticipations, unlikely as well as likely.

FMFM 1-1 ——————— Designing the Campaign

As the example shows, each phase of the campaign is generally aimed at some intermediate goal necessary to the ultimate accomplishment of the larger aim of the campaign. And as the example also shows, each phase should have a clearly understood intent of its own which contributes to the overall intent of the campaign. While we may envision each phase lasting a certain duration, the phases of a campaign are event-oriented rather than time-oriented. Each phase should represent a natural subdivision of the campaign; we should not break the campaign down into numerous arbitrary parts which can lead to a plodding, incremental approach that sacrifices tempo.

The further ahead we project, the less certain and detailed will be our designs. We may plan the initial phase of a campaign with some degree of certainty, but since the results of that phase will shape the phases that follow, subsequent plans will become increasingly general. The design for future phases may consist of no more than contingencies, options, and a general intent.

The process of developing a sequence of phases in a campaign operates in two directions, forward and backward, simultaneously. On the one hand, we begin with the current situation and plan ahead, envisioning succeeding progressive phases that build upon each other. Each phase lays the groundwork for its successor until, by this connected chain of tactical events, the stage is set for the eventual decisive action. But at the same time, we cannot devise any sequence of events without a clear vision of the final object. We must have the desired end state clearly in mind—even while recognizing its tentative nature—from which we envision a reasonable series of phases backward toward the present.

The idea of sequencing applies to resources as well as to actions. Sequencing allows us to allocate resources effectively over time. The thought of economy, or conservation, rises to the fore again: taking the long view, we must ensure that resources are available as needed in the later stages of the campaign. Effective sequencing must take into account the process of logistical culmination. If resources are insufficient to sustain the force through to the accomplishment of the strategic aim, logistics may demand that the campaign be organized into sequential phases which can be supported, each phase followed by a logistical buildup—as in the case of Eisenhower's operational pause at the Rhine. Moreover, logistical requirements may dictate the direction of operational plans. For example, one phase of Eisenhower's plan for the reconquest of Europe after the Normandy breakout was a northern thrust with Montgomery's Twenty-first Army Group to capture needed ports.

Resource availability depends in large part on time schedules, such as sustainment or deployment rates, rather than on the events of war. Therefore, as we develop our intended phases we must reconcile the time-oriented phasing of resources with the event-oriented phasing of operations.

Direction

The commander further focuses the campaign by providing an operational direction which unifies the various actions within the campaign. As a campaign generally has a single strategic aim—which establishes a strategic direction—so should it have a single operational direction which leads most directly toward that aim. We should recognize that what is strategically most direct may in fact be indirect operationally. The need to move in more than one operational direction generally warrants more than one campaign.

In the classic sense, direction equates to a line of operations along which the force advances or falls back, maneuvers and fights, and sustains itself. But direction does not apply only in the spatial sense—particularly in unconventional conflicts in which the spatial dimension seems to be less significant. Direction establishes a purposeful current of connectivity between actions which advances resolutely toward the final aim. It may be a physical axis. Or it may be a guiding manner of operating which harmonizes the phases of a campaign in purpose and makes them mutually supporting.

Where possible, we should select a variable direction which offers multiple options, or branches,[19] thus providing flexibility and ambiguity to our actions. A comparison of General Sherman's Atlanta campaign and his campaigns thereafter offers interesting insight. In his Atlanta campaign, Sherman had been hampered by the existence of a single objective, which simplified "the opponent's task in trying to parry his thrusts. This limitation Sherman now ingeniously planned to avoid by placing the opponent repeatedly 'on the horns of a dilemma'—the phrase he used to express his aim. He took a line of advance which kept the Confederates in doubt, first, whether Macon or Augusta, and then whether Augusta or Savannah was his objective. And while Sherman had his preference, he was ready to take the alternative objective if conditions favored the change."[20] Then, campaigning through the Carolinas, he opted again for a variable direction "so that his opponents could not decide whether to cover Augusta or Charleston, and their forces became divided. Then, after he had ignored both points and swept between them to gain Columbia . . . the Confederates were kept in uncertainty as to whether Sherman was aiming for Charlotte or Fayetteville. And when in turn he advanced from Fayetteville they could not tell whether Raleigh or Goldsborough was his next, and final, objective."[21]

A single operational direction does not mean that we must concentrate our forces in a single direction tactically as well. In fact, multiple tactical thrusts that are mutually enhancing increase the speed and ambiguity of our operations. Consider the German blitzes into Poland and France in 1939 and '40 which were characterized by multiple, broadly dispersed thrusts but all of which shared a common direction and were thus unified by a single focus—shattering the depth and cohesion of the enemy defenses.

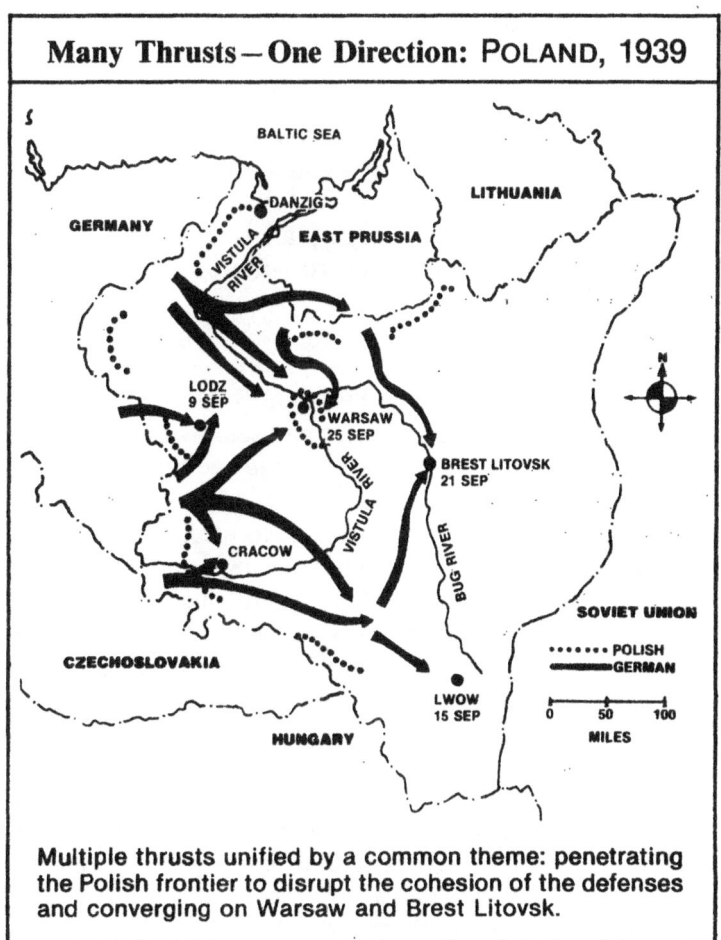

Many Thrusts — One Direction: POLAND, 1939

Multiple thrusts unified by a common theme: penetrating the Polish frontier to disrupt the cohesion of the defenses and converging on Warsaw and Brest Litovsk.

CAMPAIGN PLAN

The campaign plan is a statement of the commander's design for prosecuting his portion of the war effort, from preparation through a sequence of related operations to a well-defined end state which guarantees the attainment of the strategic aim.[22] The campaign plan is a mechanism for providing focus and direction to subordinates executing tactical missions.

The campaign plan must highlight the strategic aim. It should describe, to subordinates and seniors alike, the end state which will guarantee that aim, the overall concept and intent of the campaign, a tentative sequence of phases and operational objectives which will lead to success, and general concepts for key supporting functions, especially a logistical concept which will sustain the force throughout the campaign. The logistical concept is vital, since logistics, perhaps more than any other functional concern, can dictate what is operationally feasible.

The plan may describe the initial phases of the campaign with some certainty. But the design for succeeding phases will become increasingly general as uncertainty grows and the situation becomes increasingly unpredictable. The campaign must remain at all times flexible. However, the final phase, the anticipated decisive action which will achieve final success and toward which the entire campaign builds, should be clearly envisioned and described.[23]

FMFM 1-1 — Designing the Campaign

The campaign plan establishes tentative milestones and becomes a measure of progress, but, short of the dictates of strategy, is not a schedule in any final, immutable sense. Until the final aim is realized, we must continuously adapt our campaign plan to changing aims (ours and the enemy's), results, resources, and limiting factors. Like any plan, the campaign plan is only "a datum plane from which [we] build as necessity directs and opportunity offers."[24]

The campaign plan should be concise; General MacArthur's plan for his Southwest Pacific theater of operations was only four pages.[25] The campaign plan does not describe the execution of its phases in tactical detail. Rather, it provides guidance for developing the operations plans and orders which will in turn provide the tactical design for those phases.

Chapter 3

Conducting the Campaign

"For to win one hundred victories in one hundred battles is not the acme of skill. To subdue the enemy without fighting is the acme of skill."[1]

—Sun Tzu

"We must make this campaign an exceedingly active one. Only thus can a weaker country cope with a stronger; it must make up in activity what it lacks in strength."[2]

—Stonewall Jackson

"A prince or general can best demonstrate his genius by managing a campaign exactly to suit his objectives and his resources, doing neither too much nor too little."[3]

—Carl von Clausewitz

Having discussed designing a campaign, we now turn to the actual conduct of the campaign. This is not to say that there is a point at which design ceases and execution begins: we have already concluded that campaign design is continuous. In fact, design and conduct are interdependent: just as our design shapes our execution, so do the results of execution cause us to modify our design even in the midst of execution. Only with this thought firmly in mind can we proceed to discuss campaign execution.

Reduced to its essence, the art of campaigning consists of deciding who, when, and where to fight for what purpose. Equally important, it involves deciding who, when, and where not to fight. It is, as Clausewitz described, "the use of engagements for the object of the war."[4]

STRATEGIC ORIENTATION

As in campaign design, the overriding consideration in conducting the campaign is an unwavering focus on the requirements of the theater strategy. The aims, resources, and limitations established by strategy become the filter through which we view all our actions, even if, as at the lower echelons of command, the connection with strategy is only derivative. Even task force commanders and below, who do not function immediately at the theater level, must see their tactical decisions as derivative of the theater strategy. Consequently, the requirements of strategy must be communicated clearly to even tactical commanders.

USE OF COMBAT

Fighting, or combat, is central to war. But because tactical success of itself does not guarantee strategic success, there is an art to the way we put combat to use. We must view each envisioned action—battle, engagement, refusal to give battle, interdiction mission, feint—as an essential component of a larger whole rather than as an independent, self-contained event.

At the tactical level, clearly, the aim is to win in combat (within the parameters dictated by strategy). But the overriding influences of the strategic and operational levels may put these actions in a different context. In this way, tactical defeat can amount to strategic success, as for the North Vietnamese at Tet in 1986, while tactical victory can bring operational failure, as for Lee at Antietam.

While combat is a necessary part of war, it is by nature costly. The fuel of war is human lives and material; as Eisenhower wrote, "the word is synonymous with waste . . . The

FMFM 1-1 ——————— **Conducting the Campaign**

problem is to determine how, in time and space, to expend assets so as to achieve the maximum in results."[5] Economy thus dictates that we use combat wisely.

We do this first by fighting when it is to our advantage to do so—when we are strong compared to the enemy or we have identified some exploitable vulnerability in our enemy—and avoiding battle when we are at a disadvantage. When at a disadvantage tactically, economy means refusing to engage in battle in that particular situation. When at a tactical disadvantage theater-wide, it means waging a campaign based on hit-and-run tactics and a general refusal to give pitched battle, except when local advantage exists. This can be seen in countless historical examples: Rome under Fabius versus Hannibal, the Viet Cong in Vietnam, Washington and Nathanael Greene in the Revolutionary War, and Lettow-Vorbeck in German East Africa in the First World War.[6] By the same token, given a theater-wide advantage, we might want to bring the enemy to battle at every opportunity: Rome under Varro versus Hannibal, the United States in Vietnam, Eisenhower in Europe, or Grant versus Lee. But such a strategy is generally costly and time-consuming, and success depends on three conditions: first, that popular support for this strategy will outlast the enemy's ability to absorb attrition; second, that the enemy is willing or can be compelled to accept battle on a large scale—as Lee and the Germans were, but the Viet Cong generally were not; and third, and most important, that there is something to be gained strategically by exploiting this tactical advantage.

It is not sufficient to give battle simply because it is tactically advantageous to do so. It is more important that it be strategically advantageous or strategically necessary; that is, there should be something to gain strategically by fighting or to lose by not fighting. Strategic gain or necessity can be sufficient reason even when the situation is tactically disadvantageous. It thus is conceivable to accept or even expect a tactical defeat which serves strategy. In that way, after running away from Cornwallis' British forces for six weeks in the Carolinas in 1781, Nathanael Greene could decide "to give battle on the theory that he could hardly lose. If Cornwallis should win a tactical victory, he was already so far gone in exhaustion it would probably hurt him almost as much as a defeat."[7]

As an example of failure in this regard, consider the German offensive of March 1918—a dramatic tactical success by standards of the day—in which General Erich Ludendorff had attacked "at those points where it was easiest to break through and not at those points where the announced aim of the offensive could be served."[8] Of the March offensive, Martin van Creveld commented: "Ludendorff started from the assumption that tactics were more important than strategy; it was a question above all of launching an offensive at a point where a tactical breakthrough was possible, not where a strategic one was desirable."[9] Ludendorff's failure was not so much that he pursued tactical success, but that he did not exploit that success strategically. When at a strategic and operational disadvantage, as was Ludendorff's case, we may have to pursue the only advantage left, even if it is only tactical. The essential key, however, is to elevate the effects of tactical success to a higher level. This was Ludendorff's failure. Rather than reinforcing the Eighteenth Army, which was succeeding and might have effected an operational breakthrough, he reinforced the Seventeenth, which had been halted. So, while a tactical success, the offensive failed to achieve the desired operational penetration.

Ideally, the operational commander fights only when and where he wants to. His ability to do this is largely a function of his ability to maintain the initiative and shape the events of war to his purposes. "In war it is all-important to gain and retain the initiative, to make the enemy conform to your action, to dance to your tune."[10] And initiative in turn is largely the product of maintaining a higher operational tempo. But we must realize that we may not always be able to fight on our own terms; we may be compelled to fight by a skillful enemy who wants to fight or by strategic constraints. In such cases, we have no choice but to give battle in a way that serves strategy as much as possible and to exploit the results of combat to the greatest advantage. It is in this light that a tactical defeat may amount to a strategic victory, as for the North Vietnamese in the 1968 Tet offensive, which, although repulsed, struck a serious blow against American resolve.

The conduct of the battle, once joined, is principally a tactical problem, but even then the tactician should keep larger aims in mind as he fights. As an example, consider Guderian at the battle of Sedan, May 1940. Guderian's XIXth Panzer corps was attacking generally south "to win a bridgehead over the Meuse at Sedan and thus to help the infantry divisions that would be following to cross that river. No instructions were given as to what was to be done in the event of a surprise success."[11] By 13 May, Guderian had forced a small bridgehead. By the 14th, he had expanded the bridgehead to the south and west, but had not broken through the French defenses. Contemplating the tactical decision of how to continue the battle, without higher guidance, Guderian opted to attack west in concert with the strategic aim of the campaign. "1st and 2d Panzer Divisions received orders immediately to change direction with all their forces, to cross the Ardennes Canal, and to head west with the objective of breaking clear through the French defenses."[12]

Perspective

The operational level of war is largely a matter of perspective. The campaign demands a markedly different perspective than the battle. It requires us to *think big,* as Slim put it, seeing beyond the parameters of immediate combat to the requirements of the theater strategy as the basis for deciding when, where, and who to fight. We should view no tactical action in isolation, but always in light of the design for the theater as a whole.

Tactics Supporting Operations: GUDERIAN, 1940

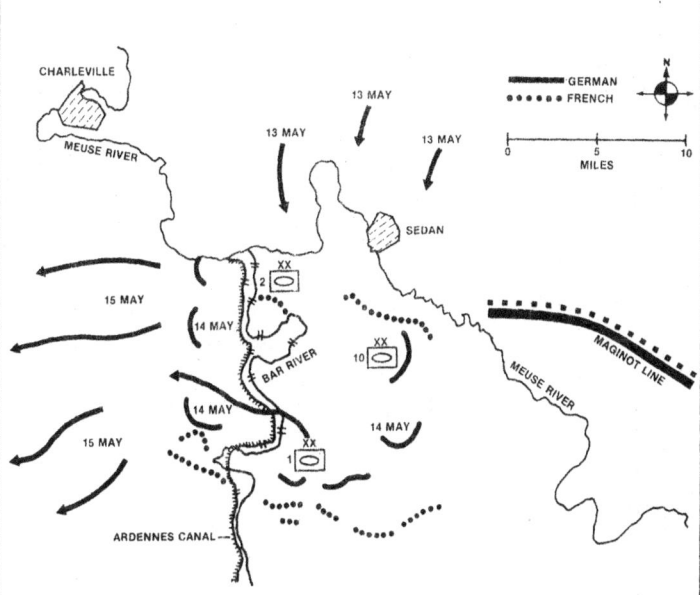

Guderian's tactical conduct of the battle of the Sedan bridgehead reflected an appreciation for the operational and strategic situations. In the midst of the battle he changed his direction of attack in keeping with the aim of the campaign: "1st and 2d Panzer Divisions received orders immediately to change direction with all their forces, to cross the Ardennes Canal, and to head west with the objective of breaking clear through the French defenses."

FMFM 1-1 ——————— Conducting the Campaign

While the tactician looks at the immediate tactical problem and the conditions directly preceding and following, the operational commander must take a broader view. He must not become so involved in tactical activities that he loses his proper perspective. This broader perspective implies broader dimensions of time and space over which to apply the military art. The actual dimensions of the operational canvas vary with the nature of the war, the size and capabilities of available forces, and the geographical characteristics of the theater. But the commander must use all the time and space within his influence to create the conditions of success. In 1809, Napoleon carried with him maps of the entire continent of Europe, thus enabling consideration of operations wherever they suited his purposes.[13] Similarly, when after five years Rome had been unable to drive Hannibal out of Italy by direct confrontation, Scipio in 204 B.C. compelled the Carthaginian to abandon Italy without a fight by opening a new front in Africa.

Given this broader perspective, the MAGTF commander can use the inherent reach of his organic aviation to see and shape the course of the campaign in time and space well in advance of the close combat of ground forces. This reach applies not only to the direct application of aviation combat power, but also to the range it provides ground forces as well. Such activities include attempting to ascertain the enemy's operational intentions; delaying enemy reinforcements by interdiction; degrading critical enemy functions or capabilities such as command and control, offensive air support, or logistics; and manipulating the enemy's perceptions.

Based on this larger perspective, the operational commander views military geography on a different scale as well. He should not be concerned with the details of terrain that are of critical importance to the tactician in combat, such as hillocks, draws, fingers, clearings or small woods, creeks, or broken trails. Rather, his concern is with major geographical features which can bear on the campaign: rivers, roads, railways, mountain ridges, towns, airfields, ports, and natural resource areas. Although by this time the German army had introduced tactical maps with contour lines showing terrain relief, for his 1866 and 1870 campaigns Moltke used railroad maps of Europe[14] — his concern was with the movement of large forces. Similarly, Patton believed that "in the higher echelons, a layered map of the whole theater to a reasonable scale, showing roads, railways, streams, and towns is more useful than a large-scale map cluttered up with ground forms and a multiplicity of nonessential information."[15]

The difference among the levels of war being one of degree, many activities in war apply universally but manifest themselves differently at the different levels. The simplest way to understand these distinctions is to use the construct we established in chapter 1 which describes activities at the strategic level as bearing directly on the war overall, at the

Campaigning ─────────────── FMFM 1-1

operational level as bearing on the campaign, and at the tactical level as bearing on combat; that is, the battle or engagement. Since a higher level in the hierarchy outweighs a lower, we should seek to give our actions impact at the highest possible level. Thus, as we mentioned, in designing our campaign we seek to attack those critical enemy factors of strategic vice operational or tactical importance. In the same way, as we will see, operational maneuver carries a greater decisive effect than tactical maneuver.

LEVEL	FUNCTION/CAPABILITY							ARENA
STRATEGY	M A N E U V E R	M O B I L I T Y	T E M P O	I N T E L L I G E N C E	S U R P R I S E	L O G I S T I C S	L E A D E R S H I P	WAR
OPERATIONS								CAMPAIGN / THEATER
TACTICS								ENGAGEMENT / BATTLE

MANEUVER

Maneuver is the employment of forces to secure an advantage — or leverage — over the enemy to accomplish the mission. Tactical maneuver aims to gain an advantage in combat. Operational maneuver, on the other hand, impacts beyond the realm of combat. In fact, it aims to reduce the amount of fighting necessary to accomplish the mission. By operational maneuver, we seek to gain an advantage which bears directly on the outcome of the campaign or in the theater as a whole. A classic example is MacArthur's landing of the 1st Marine Division at Inchon in 1950, by which he collapsed the overextended North Korean army surrounding Pusan. Another is Sherman's Atlanta campaign in 1864 in which he repeatedly refused battle, instead turning the Confederate flank successively at Dalton, Resaca, Cassville, Allatoona, Marietta (but here only after his attempted assault had failed at Kennesaw Mountain), and the Chatahoochie River. His opponent Joseph Johnston's response was to try to halt the Union advance by defending from strong battle positions (which he had had the entire winter to prepare) along the route of advance, falling back to subsequent prepared positions when necessary. By ignoring Johnston's attempts to bring him to battle, Sherman nullified the strength of Johnston's tactical defense; instead he maneuvered directly against the objective of the campaign, Atlanta.[16]

Typically, we think of maneuver as a function of relational movement and fire on a grand scale, but this is not necessarily the case. The Combined Action Program, begun by III Marine Amphibious Force under General Lewis Walt in 1965 during the Vietnam War, is an example of unconventional maneuver at the operational level. The program sought to make the Viet Cong guerrillas' position untenable by attacking their essential base of popular support through the pacification of South Vietnamese villages.

Operational Maneuver: SHERMAN, 1864

Advancing on Atlanta, Sherman refuses Johnston's repeated efforts to compel him to make frontal assaults against prepared defensive positions, instead turning the Confederate flank repeatedly.

FMFM 1-1 — Conducting the Campaign

If tactical maneuver takes place during and within battle, operational maneuver takes place before, after, and beyond battle. The operational commander seeks to secure a decisive advantage before battle is joined—as Napoleon did at Ulm in 1805 by means of a turning movement so decisive that Mack surrendered his army of 30,000 after only one half-hearted attempt to break out. Equally, the operational commander seeks to exploit tactical success to achieve strategic results—as General Sir Edmund Allenby did in Palestine and Syria in 1918 after penetrating the right wing of the Turkish line at the Battle of Megiddo. The victory at Megiddo was not decisive in itself, but was a necessary precondition for strategic success. In 38 days, Allenby had advanced 360 miles, destroyed three Turkish armies, took 76,000 prisoners, and knocked Turkey out of the war.[17] The only tactical action of the campaign was the breakthrough, during which Allenby suffered most of his 5,000 casualties; the rest was an operational pursuit. Interestingly, Allenby's original plan reflected only a tactical ambition; it would certainly have resulted in the defeat of the Turkish Eighth Army (one of three Turkish armies manning the front) but would not have unhinged the entire Turkish defense or threatened the critical Hejaz railroad. With no additional forces, Allenby used the same basic concept but modified the scope to exploit to greater depth and collapse the entire defense.

A vivid example of failure to exploit tactical opportunity is the battle of Sidi Barrani in North Africa, December 1940. In a maneuver reminiscent of Allenby in Syria, General Sir Richard O'Connor's Western Desert Force of two divisions

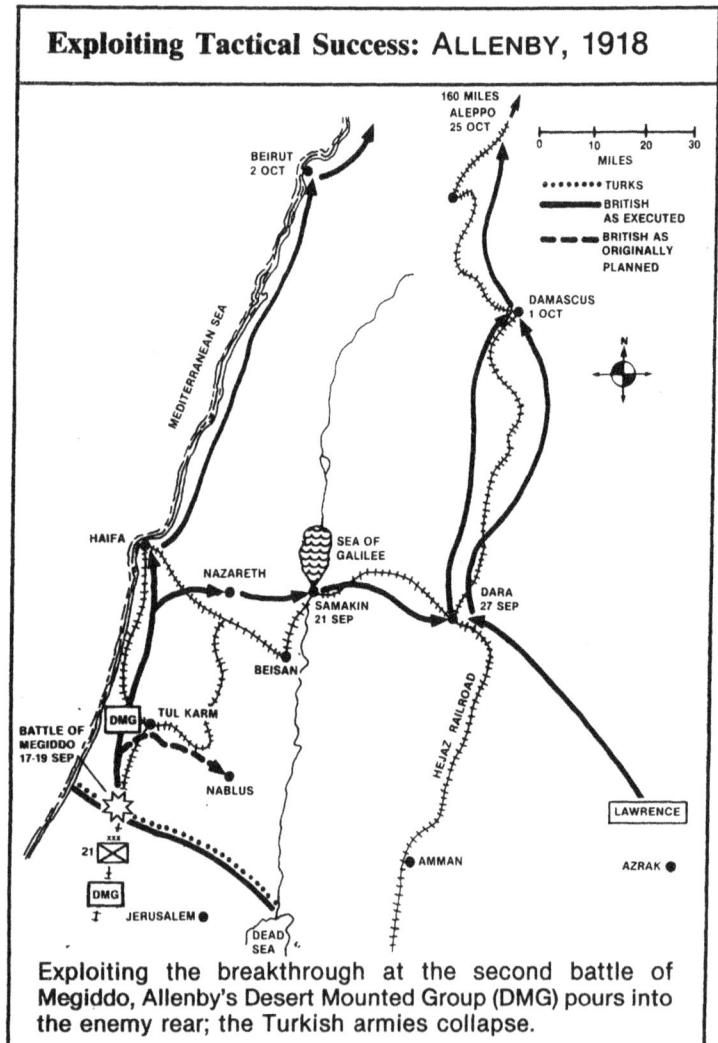

Exploiting the breakthrough at the second battle of Megiddo, Allenby's Desert Mounted Group (DMG) pours into the enemy rear; the Turkish armies collapse.

Conducting the Campaign

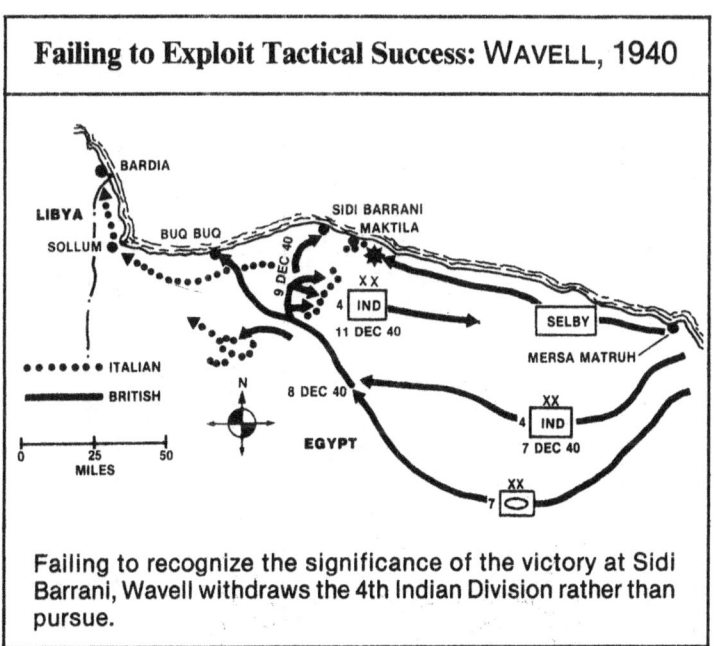

Failing to Exploit Tactical Success: WAVELL, 1940

Failing to recognize the significance of the victory at Sidi Barrani, Wavell withdraws the 4th Indian Division rather than pursue.

penetrated and collapsed a much larger Italian force. The higher commander in Cairo, General Sir Archibald Wavell, who had never envisioned the attack as anything more than a raid, promptly withdrew the 4th Indian Division for an offensive in Eritrea, forfeiting the potential opportunity to end the war in North Africa and setting the stage for the arrival of Erwin Rommel and the legend of "The Desert Fox." Liddell Hart recounted: "Thus on December 11, the third day of the battle, the routed Italians were running westwards in panic while half the victor's force was marching eastwards—back to back!"[18]

Closer to home, the Battle of the Crater at Petersburg in July 1864 illustrates the same sort of failure. Four tons of gunpowder detonated by Union forces in the Petersburg Mine tore a great gap in the Confederate defenses. Burnside's IXth Corps was to assault through the gap, but the operation was bungled, the Confederate forces rallied over time to seal the gap by fire, and 3,293 Union soldiers were lost in "one of the great tragic fiascos of the war."[19]

Carried to its perfect extreme, operational maneuver would, in Liddell Hart's words, "produce a decision without any serious fighting"[20] — as for Napoleon at Ulm. "For even if decisive battle be the goal, the aim of strategy must be to bring about this battle under the most advantageous circumstance. And the more advantageous the circumstance, the less, proportionately, will be the fighting."[21] Therefore, the *"true aim is not so much to seek battle as to seek a strategic situation so advantageous that if it does not of itself produce the decision, its continuation by a battle is sure to achieve this."*[22]

MOBILITY

If the classic application of maneuver is relational movement, then superior mobility — the capability to move from place to place while retaining the ability to perform the mission[23] — becomes a key ingredient. The object is to use mobility to develop leverage by creating superiority at the point of battle or to avoid altogether disadvantageous battle.

In maneuver at the operational level, naturally it is not tactical mobility that matters but operational mobility. The difference, if subtle, is significant. Tactical mobility is the ability to move in combat; that is, *within* the engagement or battle. Tactical mobility is a function of speed and acceleration over short distances, of protection, agility, and the ability to move cross-country. Operational mobility is the ability to move between engagements and battles within the context of the campaign or theater. Operational mobility is a function of range and sustained speed over distance.[24] If the essence of the operational level is deciding when and where to fight, operational mobility is the means by which we commit the necessary forces based on that decision. An advantage in operational mobility can have a significant impact. In the First World War, that advantage resided with the defender, who could shift forces laterally by rail faster than the attacker could advance on foot. By the Second World War, mechanization had reversed the advantage, as Germany's overrunning of France demonstrated.[25]

Tactics demand movement cross-country, but operational movement, for speed and volume, relies on existing road, rail, or river networks. Patton recognized this when he wrote: "Use roads to march on; fields to fight on . . . When the roads are available for use, you save time and effort by staying on them until shot off."[26]

Although we typically think of shipping as a component of strategic mobility, it may be employed to operational effect as well. In many cases, a MAGTF carried on amphibious shipping can enjoy greater operational mobility along a coastline than an enemy moving along the coast by roads — particularly when the amphibious force has the ability to interfere with the enemy's use of those roads. In this way, the MAGTF maneuvers by landing where the enemy is vulnerable.[27] If exploited, such an advantage in operational mobility can be decisive. Similarly, while we typically think of helicopters as a means of improving mobility tactically, we should not rule out their usefulness as a means of mobility in the operational sense as well.

TEMPO

Tempo is a rate or rhythm of activity. Tempo is a significant weapon because it is through a faster tempo that we seize the initiative and dictate the terms of war. Tactical tempo is the rate of work within an engagement. Operational tempo is the rate of work between engagements. In other words, it is the ability to consistently shift quickly from one tactical action to another.

FMFM 1-1 ——————— **Conducting the Campaign**

It is not in absolute terms that tempo matters, but in terms relative to the enemy. After his breakthrough at Megiddo, in what amounted to a rout Allenby averaged less than ten miles a day, but the tempo was more than the Turks could handle; they were never able to reconstitute their defense and return the action to the tactical level.

We create operational tempo in several ways. First, we gain tempo by multiple tactical actions undertaken simultaneously. Thus, the multiple tactical thrusts we discussed in chapter 2 as a means of creating flexibility and ambiguity also generate tempo.

Second, we gain tempo by anticipating tactical results and developing in advance *sequels* for exploiting those results without delay.

Third, we generate tempo by creating a command system based on decentralized decision-making within the framework of a unifying intent. Slim recalled of his experience in Burma in the Second World War: "Commanders at all levels had to act more on their own; they were given greater latitude to work out their own plans to achieve what they knew was the Army Commander's intention. In time they developed to a marked degree a flexibility of mind and a firmness of decision that enabled them to act swiftly to take advantage of sudden information or changing circumstances without reference to their superiors."[28]

And finally, we maintain tempo by avoiding unnecessary combat. Any battle or engagement, even if we destroy the enemy, takes time and thus saps our operational tempo. So we see another reason besides the desire for economy for fighting only when and where necessary. Conversely, by maintaining superior operational tempo we can lessen the need to resort to combat. The German blitz through France in 1940 was characterized more by the calculated avoidance of pitched battle after the breakthrough than by great tactical victories. By contrast, French doctrine called for deliberate, methodical battle. When denied this by the German tempo of operations, the defenders were overwhelmed; like the Turks versus Allenby, they were unable to reconstitute an organized resistance and force the Germans to fight for their gains.[29] Liddell Hart wrote of the 1940 campaign in France:

> The issue turned on the time-factor at stage after stage. French countermeasures were repeatedly thrown out of gear because their timing was too slow to catch up with the changing situations . . . The French commanders, trained in the slow-motion methods of 1918, were mentally unfitted to cope with the panzer pace, and it produced a spreading paralysis among them.[30]

INTELLIGENCE

The differences among the tactical, operational, and strategic levels of intelligence are principally ones of scope. Tactical intelligence provides information on the environment and enemy capabilities as they affect combat; that is, of an immediate or imminent impact. Operational intelligence provides information which impacts on the campaign; it must reflect the broader perspective of operations. Operational intelligence thus must take a wider view over area and a longer view over time. As the operational level of war is less a matter of actual fighting and more a matter of schemes and intentions, operational intelligence focuses less on current combat capabilities and more on forecasting future enemy capabilities, intentions, and options.

Because the operational level of war has as its aim the attainment of a strategic objective, operational intelligence must provide insight into the strategic situation and all factors, military and otherwise, that influence it. Most information-gathering assets organic to the MAGTF are principally tactical in scope, although by no means exclusively so. As a result, the MAGTF commander must often rely on assets external to the MAGTF for sources for much of his operational intelligence.

SURPRISE

Surprise is a state of disorientation which is the result of unexpected events and which degrades ability to react effectively. Surprise can be of decisive importance. Tactical surprise catches the enemy unprepared in such a way as to affect the outcome of combat; it is of a relatively immediate and local nature. Operational surprise catches the enemy unprepared in such a way as to impact on the campaign. To achieve operational surprise, we need not catch the enemy tactically unaware. For example, at the Inchon landing in 1950, the need for the early capture of Wolmi-do island, which dominated the inner approaches to Inchon harbor, compromised any hope of achieving tactical surprise with the main landings. But operational surprise was complete; although the assault on Wolmi-do was preceded by a five-day aerial bombardment, the North Korean army surrounding Pusan could not react in time. It was cut off and soon collapsed.[31] The subsequent entry of Communist China into the war achieved surprise of a strategic order, significantly altering the entire balance of the war.

Surprise may be the product of deception, by which we mislead the enemy into acting in a way prejudicial to his interests[32] — for example, the Normandy invasion in which an elaborate deception plan convinced the Germans the invasion would take place at Calais. Surprise may be the product of ambiguity, by which we leave the enemy confused as to our intentions through variable or multiple actions — for example, the Allied invasion of North Africa in 1942; Eisenhower's choice of a thousand miles of coastline from Casablanca to Tunis precluded the Axis forces from anticipating the actual landings. Or, surprise may simply be the product of a flair for the unexpected, such as MacArthur's stroke at Inchon.

Of the three, deception would seem to offer the greatest potential payoff because it deludes the enemy into a false move. But because it means actually convincing the enemy of a lie rather than simply leaving him confused or ignorant, deception is also the most difficult to execute. This is truer yet at the operational level than at the tactical. Due to the broader perspective of operations, operational deception must feed false information to a wider array of enemy intelligence collection means over a longer period of time. This increases the complexity of the deception effort, the need for consistency, and the risk of compromise.[33]

Allenby's Syrian campaign offers insight into the typical elaborateness of operational deception and the difference between tactical and operational surprise. For weeks before the beginning of the offensive, Allenby had put Colonel T.E. Lawrence, whose Arab force was operating far to the east, to work purchasing all the forage he could—enough for all Allenby's needs. Allenby had commandeered the largest hotel in Jerusalem, which was toward the eastern flank of his army, and had established a large mock headquarters there. Also, for weeks before the offensive, he had ordered large movements of forces behind his lines to simulate a concentration near the Dead Sea. The purpose of all this activity was to convince the Turks he meant to campaign in the east rather than the west. Finally, for tactical good measure to mislead the Turks as to the timing of the attack, he had scheduled and publicized widely a horse meet set for the same day. So convincing was the deception that, shortly before the offensive, an Indian defector who disclosed the plan to the Turks was dismissed by the Turks as an Allied ruse.

Logistics

At the operational level much more than at the tactical, logistics may determine what is possible and what is not; for "a campaign plan that cannot be logistically supported is not a plan at all, but simply an expression of fanciful wishes."[34]

Strategic logistics involves the development and stocking of war materials and their deployment from the United States to various theaters. At the opposite end of the spectrum, tactical logistics is concerned with sustaining forces in combat. It deals with the fueling, arming, and maintaining of troops and machines. Tactical logistics involves the actual performance of combat service support functions with resources immediately or imminently available—usually resident in the combat unit's trains. In order to perform these functions, the tactical commander must be provided the necessary resources. Providing these resources is the role of operational logistics.

Operational logistics thus connects the logistical efforts at the tactical and strategic levels, taking the resources supplied by strategy and making them available in sufficient amounts to the tactical commander. Logistics at the operational level takes on three basic tasks. The first is to procure locally those necessary resources not provided by strategy. We may accomplish this through support agreements with a host nation or other Services, through the local economy, or by capturing resources from the enemy, as was sometimes a consideration for the German forces in North Africa during the Second World War.

The second task is to manage often limited resources as necessary to sustain the campaign. This involves both the apportioning of resources among tactical forces based on the operational plan and the rationing of resources to ensure sustainment throughout the duration of the campaign. Thus, at the operational level much more than the tactical, logistics demands an appreciation for the expenditure of resources and the timely anticipation of requirements. While failure to anticipate logistical requirements at the tactical level can result in delays of hours or days, the same failure at the operational level can result in delays of days or weeks.

The third task is to deliver resources in the necessary amounts to the tactical forces. This involves the creation of a logistical delivery system sufficient to sustain the force throughout the length of the campaign and the breadth of the theater or area of operations. This system requires sufficient ports of entry to receive the necessary volume of resources supplied by strategy, lines of communication (land, sea, or air) and facilities sufficient to support the movement of those resources, and a fleet of vehicles or craft to do the moving. Road networks are naturally of principal concern, but they are not the only means by which to sustain the force. Particularly in Third World areas where roads may be inadequate, commanders should consider the use of railways (which can move far greater volumes of supplies than vehicles can in the same amount of time), navigable waterways, and aircraft as well.

The logistical system organic to a MAGTF is primarily tactical in nature, designed to support the MAGTF within the confines of the beachhead. Thus, the MAGTF commander waging a campaign beyond the beachhead must construct a logistical apparatus primarily from external sources, such as through host nation support, inter-Service agreements, or local procurement. Furthermore, the advertised 60- and 30-day logistical capability of the MEF and MEB respectively will vary depending on the nature and scope of operations, particularly if the MAGTF launches an expeditionary campaign beyond the beachhead.

Historically, American strategy has often sought to obviate the first two tasks by providing operational commanders a superabundance of resources, making the distribution of these resources the only logistical concern at the operational level. However, in expeditionary warfare, this approach is infeasible without a large-scale commitment which may be politically unacceptable. Moreover, in expeditionary warfare, this approach may not even be desirable. A large logistical base to which the combat forces are tied becomes a vulnerability which must be protected and can also limit operational freedom. The concepts of seabasing and selective off-loading, in which limited resources are transferred ashore, can alleviate this problem. The real solution is to be able to operate without a cumbersome logistical tail. Forces able to operate on a shoestring are less vulnerable to attacks against their logistical tails, are less dependent on a continuous high-volume logistical flow, and can operate on lines which would not support a large logistical apparatus. Consider again the example of Sherman, having captured Atlanta and establishing a forward base there. Future offensive action was restricted by the need to protect his 400-mile line of communication to Nashville, which was being harassed continuously by Confederate cavalry. Sherman concluded that to try to track down the elusive Confederates would be counterproductive to Grant's strategy. His solution was to reduce the size of his force by returning the Army of the Cumberland to Nashville, abandon his line of communication, and continue the advance—his "March to the Sea"—living off the countryside and making "Georgia howl."[35]

Inherent in the ability to operate this way is the willingness to sacrifice the level of luxury to which American forces have often become accustomed.

Leadership

Leadership is the personal ability to influence the performance of human beings in pursuit of a goal. The result of strong leadership is increased understanding and commitment from the members of the organization. At the higher levels of command, leadership is much less a matter of direct personal example and intervention than it is a matter of being able to energize and unify the efforts of large groups of people, sometimes dispersed over great distances. This is not to say that personal contact is unimportant at this level. Even at the highest levels, the commander must see and be seen by his Marines. As the supreme Allied commander in Europe, Eisenhower spent a great deal of time traveling throughout the theater being seen by his men. Nor does this imply that the higher commander does not intervene in the actions of his subordinates when necessary. But just as the operational level involves being able to decide when and where to fight, leadership at this level involves the ability to determine when and where personal influence is required. Since the higher commander cannot be in all places at once, he must pick his spots carefully. Finally, this is not to say that charisma and strength of personality are unimportant at this level. In fact, we might argue that because the operational commander must influence more people spread over greater distances, he should be correspondingly more charismatic and stronger of personality.

Leadership at the operational level requires clarity of vision, strength of will, and extreme moral courage—as

FMFM 1-1 — Conducting the Campaign

demonstrated repeatedly by men such as MacArthur, Slim, and Manstein. Moreover, it requires the ability to communicate these traits clearly and powerfully through numerous layers of command, each of which exerts a certain friction on effective communication. As Slim said, the operational commander must possess "the power to make his intentions clear right through the force."[36] "The will of Frederick and Napoleon," Hans von Seekt wrote, "was a living force in the humblest grenadier."[37]

The operational commander must establish a climate of cohesion among the widely dispersed elements of his command and with adjacent and higher headquarters as well.[38] Because he cannot become overly involved in tactics, the operational commander must have confidence in his subordinate commanders with whom he must develop mutual trust and an implicit understanding.

The nature of theater operations places certain peculiar demands on leadership. These will be felt most keenly by the MAGTF commander, who must coordinate externally with other Services and nationalities. He must maintain effective relationships with external organizations — particularly when other cultures are involved.[39] He must have the ability to gain consensus for joint or combined concepts of operations.[40] And he must be able to represent the capabilities, limitations, and external support requirements of the MAGTF effectively to higher headquarters.

Conclusion

"Those who know when to fight and when not to fight are victorious. Those who discern when to use many or few troops are victorious. Those whose upper and lower ranks have the same desire are victorious. Those who face the unprepared with preparation are victorious. Those whose generals are able and are not constrained by their governments are victorious." [1]

—Sun Tzu

At the risk of belaboring a point, we will repeat for the last time that tactical success of itself does not necessarily bring strategic success. "It is possible to win all the battles and still lose the war. If the battles do not lead to the achievement of the strategic objective, then, successful or not, they are just so much wasted effort."[2] Strategic success, which attains the objectives of policy, is the military object in war. Thus we recognize the need for a discipline of the military art which synthesizes tactical results to create the military conditions that induce strategic success. We have discussed the campaign as the principal vehicle by which we accomplish this synthesis.

Understandably perhaps, as tactics has long been a Marine Corps strength, we have tended to focus on the tactical aspects of war to the neglect of the operational aspects. This neglect may be further caused by the often contradictory virtues of the two levels: the headlong tactical focus on winning in combat (and the spoiling-for-a-fight mentality it necessarily promotes) compared to the operational desire to use combat sparingly. But, as we have seen, actions at the higher levels tend to overpower actions at the lower levels in the hierarchy of war, and neglect of the operational level can prove disastrous even in the face of tactical competence. In the absence of an operational design which synthesizes tactical results into a coalescent whole, what passes for operations is simply the accumulation of tactical victories.

Historically, this is not altogether uncommon.[3] As the Vietnam experience shows, even many tactical successes do not always lead to victory.

Tactical competence can rarely attain victory in the face of outright operational incompetence, while operational ignorance can squander what tactical hard work has gained. As the price of war is human loss, it is incumbent on every commander to attain his objective as economically as possible. This demands the judicious and effective use of combat, which in turn demands a skill for the conduct of war at the operational level.

The Campaign

1. Henri Jomini, *The Art of War* (Westport, CT: Greenwood Press, 1971), p. 178. What Jomini describes as strategic would be classified as operational by today's construct.

2. B.H. Liddell Hart, *Strategy* (New York: Signet Books, 1967), p. 324.

3. *The Memoirs of Field-Marshal Montgomery* (New York: World Publishing Co., 1958), p. 197.

4. Liddell Hart, *Strategy,* p. 338.

5. JCS Pub. 1-02: "**National Strategy** — (DOD, IADB) The art and science of developing and using the political, economic, and psychological powers of a nation, together with its armed forces, during peace and war, to secure national objectives." The term *national* strategy may be misleading to some since it often connotes a global perspective. Clearly, the need to coordinate all the elements of national power exists at the regional or theater level as well, and so the term *grand* strategy may be more useful.

6. JCS Pub. 1-02: "**Military Strategy** — (DOD, IADB) The art and science of employing the armed forces of a nation to secure the objectives of national policy by the application of force or the threat of force." And: "**Strategic Level of War** — (DOD) The level of war at which a nation or group of nations determines national or alliance security objectives and develops and uses national resources to accomplish those objectives. Activities at this level establish national and alliance military objectives;

sequence initiatives; define limits and assess risks for the use of military and other instruments of power; develop global or theater war plans to achieve these objectives; and provide armed forces and other capabilities in accordance with the strategic plan."

7. JCS Pub. 1-02: "**Strategic Concept**—(DOD, NATO, IADB) The course of action accepted as the result of the estimate of the strategic situation. It is a statement of what is to be done in broad terms sufficiently flexible to permit its use in framing the military, diplomatic, economic, psychological and other measures which stem from it." (Sometimes itself referred to as a "strategy.")

8. JCS Pub. 1-02: "**Tactical Level of War**—(DOD) The level of war at which battles and engagements are planned and executed to accomplish military objectives assigned to tactical units or task forces. Activities at this level focus on the ordered arrangement and maneuver of combat elements in relation to each other and to the enemy to achieve combat objectives."

9. JCS Pub. 1-02: "**Operational Level of War**—(DOD) The level of war at which campaigns and major operations are planned, conducted, and sustained to accomplish strategic objectives within theaters or areas of operations. Activities at this level link tactics and strategy by establishing operational objectives needed to accomplish the strategic objectives, sequencing events to achieve the operational objectives, initiating actions, and applying resources to bring about and sustain these events. These activities imply a broader dimension of time or space than do tactics; they ensure the logistic and administrative support of tactical forces, and provide the means by which tactical successes are exploited to achieve strategic objectives."

10. FM 100-6 (Coordinating Draft), *Large Unit Operations* (Fort Leavenworth, KS: U.S. Army Command and General Staff College, 1987), p. vii.

11. Erich von Manstein, *Lost Victories* (Novato, CA: Presidio Press, 1982), p. 79.

12. David G. Chandler, *The Campaigns of Napoleon* (New York: MacMillan Publishing Co., 1966), p. 861.

13. FM 100-6, p. 1-3.

14. *Ibid.*, p. 1-5.

15. David Jablonsky, "Strategy and the Operational Level of War," *The Operational Art of Warfare Across the Spectrum of Conflict* (Carlisle, PA: U.S. Army War College, 1987), p. 5.

16. FM 100-6, p. 1-3.

17. *Ibid.*, p. 1-4.

18. *Ibid.*

19. Carl von Clausewitz, *On War*, trans. and ed. M. Howard and P. Paret (Princeton University Press, 1984), p. 607. "No other possibility exists, then, than to subordinate the military point of view to the political."

20. Manstein: "There are admittedly cases where a senior commander cannot reconcile it with his responsibilities to carry out an order he has been given. Then, like Seydlitz at the Battle of

Zorndorf, he has to say, 'After the battle the king may dispose of my head as he will, but during the battle he will kindly allow me to make use of it.' No general can vindicate his loss of a battle by claiming that he was compelled—against his better judgment—to execute an order that led to defeat. In this case the only course open to him is that of disobedience, for which he is answerable with his head. Success will usually decide whether he was right or not." *Lost Victories*, pp. 361-2.

21. FM 100-6, p. vii.

22. Sun Tzu, *The Art of War*, trans. Samuel B. Griffith (New York: Oxford University Press, 1971), p. 93.

23. Jablonsky, p. 11.

24. John F. Meehan III, "The Operational Trilogy," *Parameters*, vol. XVI, no. 3 (September 1986), p. 13.

25. See Edward N. Luttwak, *Strategy: The Logic of War and Peace* (Cambridge, MA: Harvard University Press, 1987), pp. 69-71, 208-230.

26. By comparison, consider the equally successful German, Gen. Paul von Lettow-Vorbeck, in the First World War in German East Africa, who wrote in his memoirs: "Owing to the position of German East Africa and the weakness of the existing forces—the peace establishment was but little more than two thousand—we could only play a subsidiary part. I knew that the fate of the colonies, as of all other German possessions, would be decided only on the battlefields of Europe. The question was

whether it was possible for us in our subsidiary theatre of war to exercise any influence on the great decision at home. Could we, with our small forces, prevent considerable numbers of the enemy from intervening in Europe, or in other more important theatres, or inflict on our enemies any loss of personnel or war material worth mentioning?" *East African Campaigns* (New York: Robert Speller & Sons, 1957), p. 1.

27. See J.F.C. Fuller, *Grant and Lee: A Study in Personality and Generalship* (Bloomington, IN: Indiana University Press, 1982). Particularly pp. 242-283.

28. Russell F. Weigley, *The American Way of War* (Bloomington, IN: Indiana University Press, 1973), p. 92.

29. Ulysses S. Grant, *Personal Memoirs* (New York: Da Capo Press, 1982), p. 369.

30. *Ibid.*, p. 469.

31. Fuller, pp. 79-80.

32. Weigley, p. 118. Fuller, p. 253.

33. Weigley, p. 139.

34. *Ibid.*, p. 108

35. *Ibid.*, p. 123.

36. Grant, p. 384.

37. Fuller, p. 268. "In this respect there is no difference between Grant and Lee; neither understood the full powers of the rifle or the rifled gun; neither introduced a single tactical innovation of importance, and though the rifle tactics of the South were superior to those of the North, whilst the artillery tactics of the North were superior to those of the South, these differences were due to circumstances outside generalship."

38. L.D. Holder, "Operational Art in the US Army: A New Vigor," *Essays on Strategy*, vol. III (Washington: National Defense University Press, 1986), p. 129.

39. Weigley, p. 32. "Cornwallis arrived at the Dan worn to a frazzle, 500 men of 2,500 having dropped out since Ramsour's Mills, haversacks empty, and the Carolina partisans stripping away provisions from the countryside in their rear."

40. Contrary to Clausewitz, who describes the battle as "primarily an end in itself." He writes: "But since the essence of war is fighting, and since the battle is the fight of the main force, the battle must always be considered as the true center of gravity of the war. All in all, therefore, its distinguishing feature is that, more than any other type of action, battle exists for its own sake alone." *On War*, p. 248.

41. Liddell Hart, *Strategy*, p. 324.

42. In fact, they can be quite small; for example, the killing of Haitian guerrilla leader Charlemagne Peralte by two Marine noncommissioned officers in 1919. During this period, U.S. Marines were involved in the occupation of Haiti. Peralte had raised a rebel force of as many as five thousand in the northern

part of the country. From February through October, Marine forces pursued the rebels, known as *cacos*, fighting 131 engagements but unable to suppress the rebel activity. So, disguised as *cacos*, Sgt. Herman Hannekan and Cpl. William Button infiltrated Peralte's camp, where Hannekan shot and killed the *caco* leader. The rebellion in the north subsided. In this case, a special operation consisting of two Marines accomplished what seven months of combat could not.

Designing the Campaign

1. Attributed.

2. *On War*, p. 182.

3. *Strategy*, p. 330.

4. Meehan, p. 15.

5. Grant, p. 374.

6. Dwight D. Eisenhower, *Crusade in Europe* (New York: Da Capo Press, Inc., 1979), p. 225.

7. William S. Lind, "The Operational Art," *Marine Corps Gazette* (April 1988), p. 45.

8. Sun Tzu, p. 134.

9. Grant, p. 366.

10. But as this gift for conceptual design is the truly creative aspect of the military art, it is precisely this skill which has often been lacking. At the present, the Marine Corps as an institution devotes more time and effort to training officers in the procedural aspects of command and staff action than to developing intuitive, creative commanders — an error that must be remedied. This creative ability is generally an innate gift which can be developed in an individual to some extent, but not created. Part of the solution may be to institutionalize a method whereby we identify and develop such individuals as commanders.

11. Clausewitz, p. 77.

12. Winston S. Churchill, *The World Crisis* (New York: Charles Scribner's Sons, 1923) vol. II, p. 5.

13. Consider as an analogy the designing of an automobile. The conceptual design establishes the overall features of the car: for example, we decide that (within our appreciation for current technical capabilities) we want a small sportscar with a certain general shape, certain performance capabilities, evoking a certain image, and appealing to a certain market. This concept becomes the theme for all subsequent design. We proceed to functional design, by which we design the necessary functional components within the parameters established by the concept: the engine, the suspension system, the body, the interior, and so on. In the process, we may discover that in designing the engine we cannot achieve the desired horsepower given the size, weight, or shape of the car established in the concept. It becomes necessary

to modify the concept by adjusting the required performance or the size or shape. Finally, within the parameters of the concept and functional requirements, detailed design provides the specifications to which the car is actually built; literally, the nuts and bolts that hold the car together.

14. Eisenhower, p. 256.

15. *Ibid.*, pp. 228-9.

16. *Ibid.*, p. 229.

17. Holder, p. 124.

18. Eisenhower, p. 176. Also: "In committing troops to battle there are certain minimum objectives to be attained, else the operation is a failure. Beyond this lies the realm of reasonable expectation, while still further beyond lies the realm of hope—all that might happen if fortune persistently smiles upon us.

"A battle plan normally attempts to provide guidance even into this final area, so that no opportunity for extensive exploitation may be lost . . .", p. 256.

19. Holder, p. 123.

20. Liddell Hart, *Strategy*, p. 134.

21. *Ibid.*, pp. 134-5.

22. William W. Mendel and Floyd T. Banks, "Campaign Planning: Getting It Straight," *Parameters*, vol. XVIII, no. 3 (September 1988), p. 45. From JCS Pub. 1-02: "**Campaign Plan**—(DOD, IADB) A plan for a series of related military operations aimed to accomplish a common objective, normally within a given time and space."

23. Mendel and Banks, p. 45.

24. George S. Patton, Jr., *War As I Knew It* (New York: Bantam Books, 1980), p. 374.

25. Meehan, p. 15.

Conducting the Campaign

1. Sun Tzu, *The Art of War*, p. 77.

2. In a letter, April 1863, as quoted in Robert D. Heinl, Jr., *Dictionary of Military and Naval Quotations* (Annapolis, MD: U.S. Naval Academy, 1978) p. 1.

3. Clausewitz, *On War*, p. 177.

4. *Ibid.*, p. 128.

5. Eisenhower, p. 119.

6. After a successful but costly tactical action, Lettow-Vorbeck concluded: "Although the attack carried out at Jassini with nine companies had been completely successful, it showed that such heavy losses as we also had suffered could only be borne in exceptional cases. We had to economize our forces in order to last out a long war . . . The need to strike great blows only quite exceptionally, and to restrict myself principally to guerilla warfare, was evidently imperative.", pp. 56-57.

7. Weigley, p. 32.

8. Gordon A. Craig, "Delbrueck: The Military Historian," *Makers of Modern Strategy from Machiavelli to the Nuclear Age*, ed. Peter Paret (Princeton, NJ: Princeton University Press, 1986) p. 351. As quoted by William J. Bolt and David Jablonsky, "Tactics and the Operational Level of War," *The Operational Level of War Across the Spectrum of Conflict* (Carlisle, PA: U.S. Army War College, 1987), p. 38.

9. Martin van Creveld, *Command in War*, (Cambridge, MA: Harvard University Press, 1985), p. 172.

10. Sir William Slim, *Defeat Into Victory* (London: Cassell and Company, 1956), p. 292.

11. Heinz Guderian, *Panzer Leader* (Washington: Zenger Publishing, 1952), p. 97.

12. *Ibid.*, pp. 105-106.

13. van Creveld, p. 290.

14. Interview 1 Nov 89 with Bruce I. Gudmundsson, author of *Storm Troop Tactics* (New York: Praeger, 1989).

15. Patton, pp. 373-374. From this reasoning we might conclude that a 1:50,000 map, which clearly shows terrain in tactical detail and therefore promotes a tactical perspective, is in many cases inappropriate at the MAGTF level.

16. R. Ernest and Trevor N. Dupuy, *Encyclopedia of Military History*, 2d revised edition (New York: Harper & Row, 1986), pp. 898-900.

17. *Ibid.*, p. 988.

18. B.H. Liddell Hart, *History of the Second World War* (New York: G.P. Putnam's Sons, 1970), p. 114. Ironically, Wavell, who had been with Allenby in the First World War, wrote shortly before the offensive: "It is, however, possible that an opportunity may offer for converting the enemy's defeat into an outstanding victory. . . . I do wish to make certain that if a big opportunity occurs we are prepared morally, mentally and administratively to use it to the fullest." Correlli Barnett, *The Desert Generals* (Bloomington, IN: Indiana University Press, 1986), p. 35.

19. Dupuy and Dupuy, p. 896. Grant, pp. 467-8.

20. Liddell Hart, *Strategy*, p. 324.

21. *Ibid.* What Liddell Hart referred to as strategy in his two-part construct of strategy-tactics, we refer to today in the strategy-operations-tactics construct as the operational level.

22. Liddell Hart, *Strategy*, p. 326. Italics in the original.

23. JCS Pub. 1-02: "**Mobility**—(DOD, NATO, IADB) A quality or capability of military forces which permits them to move from place to place while retaining the ability to fulfill their primary mission."

24. In this respect, the M1 tank, for example, with its speed, acceleration, armor, and agility has greater tactical mobility than the M60 in a tank-versus-tank comparison. But the M60 has superior operational mobility because it uses less fuel and has a greater cruising radius and because, being less complex, it demands less maintenance. Incidently, the M60 also has greater strategic mobility because, being lighter and smaller, it can be transported in greater numbers between theaters. The light armored vehicle has less tactical mobility than either tank in most environments but has operational and strategic mobility far superior to both. It can be transported in far greater numbers by strategic lift. Its comparatively simple automotive system, fuel efficiency, and wheels give it far greater operational range and speed.

25. Lind, p. 46.

26. Patton, pp. 380-381.

27. Lind, p. 46.

28. Slim, pp. 451-2.

29. See Robert A. Doughty, *The Seeds of Disaster: The Development of French Army Doctrine 1919-1939* (Hamden, CT: Archon Books, 1985), p. 4.

30. Liddell Hart, *History of the Second World War*, pp. 73-4.

31. In *Semper Fidelis: The History of the United States Marine Corps*, Allan R. Millett writes: "Although hardly an artistic success, the Inchon landing caught the NKPA [North Korean People's Army] by surprise, and by early morning of September 16 there was no doubt that the 1st Division was ready to exploit the landing. With adequate tanks, artillery, and service units ashore and covered by carrier air, the 1st Division started down the highway for Seoul.

"In five days of textbook campaigning, the 1st Marine Division closed on the approaches of Seoul by September 20." (New York: Macmillan Publishing Co.), p. 488.

32. JCS Pub. 1-02: "**Deception**—(DOD, NATO, IADB) Those measures designed to mislead the enemy by manipulation, distortion, or falsification of evidence to induce him to act in a manner prejudicial to his interests."

33. See FM 100-6, pp. 3-19 through 3-23.

34. Meehan, p. 16.

35. Dupuy and Dupuy, p. 900. Also, William T. Sherman, *Memoirs of General William T. Sherman* (New York: Da Capo Press, 1984), vol. II, p. 152.

36. Slim, p. 542.

37. Hans von Seekt, *Thoughts of a Soldier*, trans. G. Waterhouse (London: Ernest Benn Ltd., 1930), pp. 128-9.

38. FM 100-6, p. 3-23.

39. *Ibid.*, p. 3-24.

40. *Ibid.*

Conclusion

1. Sun Tzu, *The Art of War*, (abridged audio cassette), trans. by Thomas Cleary (Boston: Shambala Publications, 1989), side 1.

2. Meehan, p.15.

3. Lind, p. 45.

☆U.S. GOVERNMENT PRINTING OFFICE:1 9 9 0 -2 5 6 -9 4 5/ 2 0 0 4 1

(reverse blank)

www.ingramcontent.com/pod-product-compliance
Lightning Source LLC
Chambersburg PA
CBHW030001050426
42451CB00006B/82